Practical
Campus English

Daily Life

DARAKWON

Table of Contents

01 Nice to meet you!

Vocabulary

majored	introduce	last name	job	semester
freshman	sophomore	nationality	first name	greeting

Complete the sentences with vocabulary words.

1. I am a ________________ studying computer science at the University of California in LA.
   저는 UCLA에서 컴퓨터 공학을 전공하는 1학년생입니다.

2. She ________________ in Business Administration in college.
   그녀는 대학에서 경영학을 전공했습니다.

3. The first ________________ starts in March and finishes in July.
   첫 학기는 3월에 시작해서 7월에 끝납니다.

4. Korean women don't use their husband's ________________ after they are married.
   한국 여성은 결혼한 후에 남편의 성(姓)을 사용하지 않습니다.

5. His ________________ is to keep people safe, he is a police officer.
   그의 직업은 사람들을 안전하게 지키는 경찰관입니다.

6. Please write down your name, ________________, and passport number on this card.
   이 카드에 이름과 국적, 여권번호를 기입해 주십시오.

7. I'd like to ________________ you to my friend.
   당신을 제 친구에게 소개시켜주고 싶습니다.

8. He will become a ________________ next spring in his second year at university.
   그는 내년 봄에 대학 2학년으로 진급할 것입니다.

9. Her ________________ was Mary. I don't know what her surname was.
   그녀의 이름은 Mary였는데, 성은 모르겠습니다.

10. She smiled and gave me a warm ________________.
    그녀는 미소를 지으면서 나에게 인사를 했습니다.

Ⓐ Complete the table.

salesperson	business administration	public servant
travel agent	architecture	computer science
civil engineer	electronics	accounting
secretary	public administration	architect

Major	Job

Ⓑ Complete the card with your personal details.

Name:

Major:

Cell Phone Number:

E-mail Address:

Ⓒ Complete the self-introduction after listening to the speaker. ⟨ Track 1 ⟩

Hello. I'm ___________________.

My ___________________ is Catherine.

I'm ___________________ Korea.

I was ___________________ in Seoul in 1989.

I'm twenty-one years old.

I am a student at BC College.

My ___________________ is Business Administration.

My hobbies are using the Internet, playing soccer, and ___________________.

A **Look at the business card and answer the questions.**

> **Jane White**
> **Manager**
> **Tel: (02) 123-4567 ext. 320**
> **Fax: (02) 765-4321**
> **C.P.: 010-987-6543**
> **Jane90@eltschool.com**

1. What is her last name? _______________
2. What is her extension? _______________
3. What is her office number? _______________
4. What is her fax number? _______________

B **Match the phrases to make complete sentences.**

1. A travel agent	a. does office work such as arranging meetings.
2. A bank teller	b. makes plane and hotel reservations.
3. A computer programmer	c. deposits and withdraws money for people.
4. A secretary	d. makes software programs.
5. An accountant	e. is able to work well with numbers.

C **Listen to the statements and then fill in the blanks.** Track 2

1.

Country	Famous Product
_______________	
Nationality	
Chilean	

2.

Country	Famous Product
_______________	
Nationality	
Belgian	

3.

Country	Famous Product
Colombia	
Nationality	
_______________	

4.

Country	Famous Product
_______________	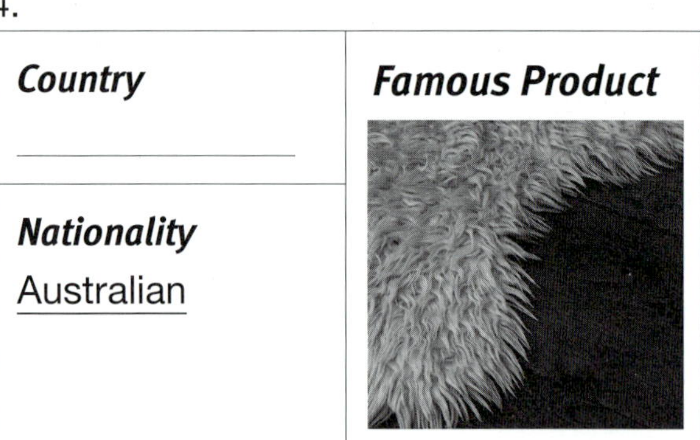
Nationality	
Australian	

D Match the questions with the answers.

1. What do you do?
2. Where do you go to school?
3. What is your first name?
4. What is your major?
5. Where is your hometown?
6. What is your e-mail address?

a. It's student@bc.ac.kr.
b. My first name is Yeona.
c. My major is accounting.
d. My hometown is Bucheon.
e. I go to Seoul University.
f. I'm a student.

E Are these good questions or not for a first meeting?

1. Do you like sports?   Good / Not good
2. How old are you?   Good / Not good
3. What do you do in your spare time?   Good / Not good
4. What's your religion?   Good / Not good
5. Are you married?   Good / Not good

F Listen to the conversation and complete the application form. Track 3

GOOD ENOUGH DEPARTMENT STORE
CREDIT CARD APPLICATION FORM

☐ NAME ________________________ ________________________
              (First)   (Last)

☐ DATE OF BIRTH __________ __________ __________
                    (Month)   (Day)   (Year)

☐ HOME ADDRESS ____

   CITY __________ STATE __________ ZIP CODE __________

☐ TELEPHONE (   ) ________________________________

☐ OCCUPATION ____

Read the passage.

Koreans and Westerners often greet people in similar ways. First, they usually say, "Hello, Nice to meet you." or something like that. Then, they ask the new person some questions.

Koreans and Westerners often ask very different questions, though. For example, Koreans often ask people very personal questions. At a first meeting, a Korean might ask questions like these: How old are you?, What's your religion?, Are you married? To a Korean, these are normal questions.

But to some Westerners, these questions may be a little impolite. Many Westerners avoid asking very personal questions when they first meet someone. So they usually do NOT ask people about their age, weight, religion, political beliefs, or even their families. Every country's culture is different. Polite questions in one culture may be impolite in another. It is important to remember which questions are polite and which questions are rude when you meet someone from another country.

 Answer the following sentences with T (true) or F (false).

1. Questions about age during a first meeting are okay with Koreans. ☐ T ☐ F
2. All Westerners dislike personal questions. ☐ T ☐ F
3. Americans might not like questions about family during a first meeting. ☐ T ☐ F

A Choose the statement which best describes what you see in the picture. Track 4

(A)   (B)   (C)   (D)

B Listen to the question and choose the best answer. Track 5

1. (A)   (B)   (C)
2. (A)   (B)   (C)
3. (A)   (B)   (C)

C Choose the best answer to each question after listening to the conversation. Track 6

4. Which year is the woman in?

(A) She's a first-year student.   (B) She's a sophomore.
(C) She's in Business Administration.   (D) She's in a city.

5. Which statement is true?

(A) He is a sophomore.   (B) She is senior to him.
(C) His major is computer engineering.   (D) She's in business now.

02 Family

 Vocabulary

relative	uncle	aunt	grandson	grandparents
personality	appearance	height	weight	siblings

Complete the sentences with vocabulary words.

1. My _______________'s birthday was on Tuesday.
   내 손자의 생일은 화요일이었다.

2. To control your _______________ you should change your eating habits and get some exercise.
   체중 조절을 위해서는 식습관을 바꾸고 운동을 해야만 합니다.

3. Her _______________ is a television presenter.
   그녀의 이모는 TV 진행자입니다.

4. My _______________ and cousins wished him good health and a long life.
   나의 삼촌과 사촌들은 그의 건강과 장수를 기원했다.

5. His _______________ is gentle and kind.
   그의 성격은 온화하고 친절하다.

6. A person's physical _______________ includes facial expressions and body type.
   사람의 신체적 외모는 표정과 체형을 포함한다.

7. She's of medium _______________, just a little shorter than you are.
   그녀는 중간 키고, 당신보다 약간 작습니다.

8. She is a very distant _______________ of mine.
   그녀는 제 아주 먼 친척입니다.

9. Many of his _______________ are jazz musicians, too.
   그의 형제자매들도 재즈 음악가입니다.

10. I want to create society where we respect our parents and _______________.
   저는 우리가 우리의 부모와 조부모를 존경하는 그런 사회를 만들고 싶습니다.

Ⓐ Complete the family tree.

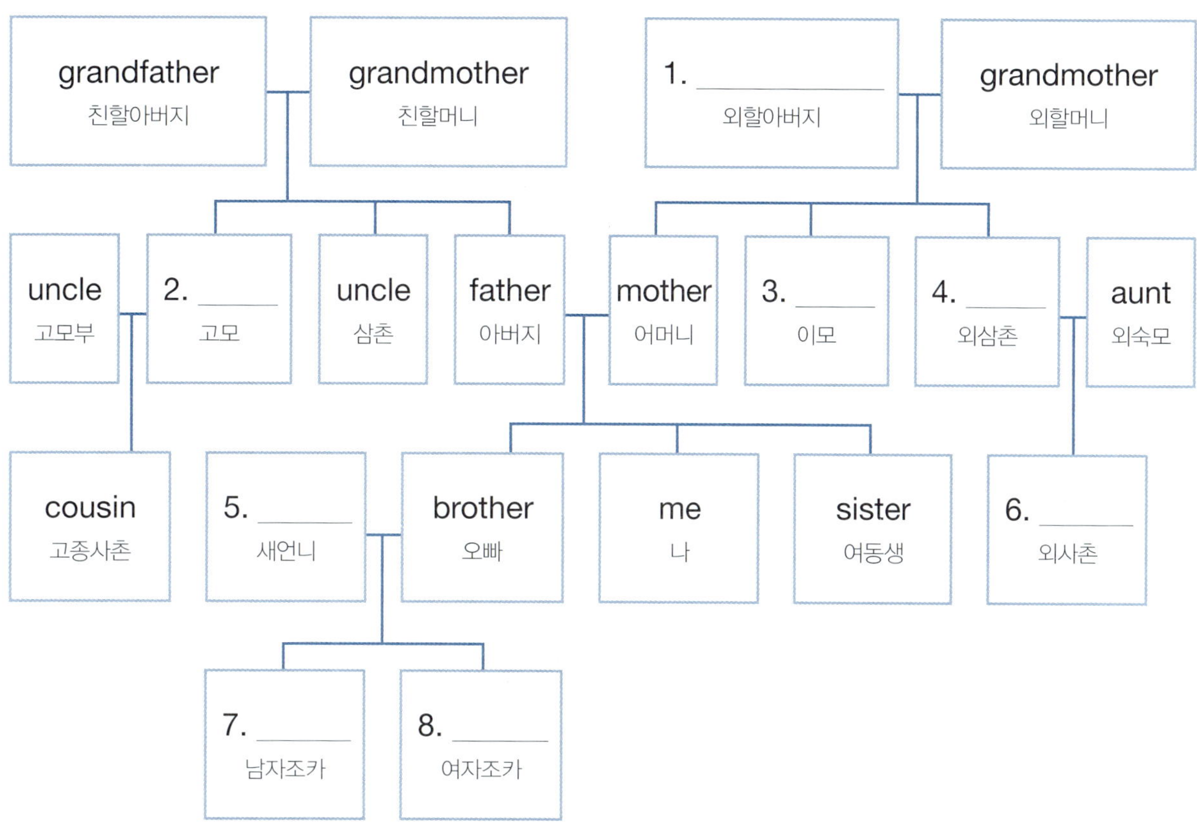

Ⓑ Listen. Which of the pictures shows the person? 🎧 Track 7

1.

2.

3.

A   **Complete the following activity based on your own appearance.**

Height	☐ tall	☐ average	☐ short
Weight	☐ thin	☐ average	☐ heavy
Eye color	☐ blue	☐ brown	☐ black
Hair length	☐ short	☐ medium	☐ long
Hair color	☐ blond	☐ brown	☐ black

B   **Use family vocabulary to complete the paragraph.**

I have two sisters, and one brother. My siblings and I all live with our parents, my aunt Jamie and my grandmother. My grandmother is my mother's ________________. Aunt Jamie is my mother's younger ________________. Aunt Jamie has a son, Tom. He lives in Japan. Tom is my mother's ________________. My older sister Sandy has a daughter, Maria. She's a baby girl. She's my ________________.

C   **Listen to the conversation and choose the correct picture.**   Track 8

1.

2.

3.

4.

D   **Circle words that describe your personality.**

friendly	talkative	outgoing	quiet	sensitive
funny	shy	serious	sincere	boring
fashionable	kind	polite	interesting	lazy
generous	intellectual	modest	energetic	diligent

E   **Listen to the conversation and complete the table.** Track 9

Who	Age	Job
grandmother	82	retired
		public servant
mother		
	25	
me		student

F   **Listen to the statement and complete the activity with family vocabulary.** Track 10

Family | 13

 **Read the passage.**

Families are important to both Koreans and Westerners. However, talking about families can be quite different in Korean and English. One big difference is the words people use to talk about their relatives.

In Korean, there are many different words for relatives. For example, in Korean, it is important to indicate if your aunt is your father's or mother's sister. But in English, people just say, "She's my aunt." The exact relationship is not important. This is even true of in-laws. In English, people just say "mother-in-law," but there are two words (Jangmo, Sieomeoni) for that relationship in Korean.

Of course, English also has ways to indicate the exact relationship between two people. For example, you could call your aunt your "father's sister" or your "mother's sister." Another common expression is to say: "She's from my father's (mother's) side of the family."

Many Westerners do not differentiate between their father's and mother's families, though. They just say aunt, uncle, grandmother, grandfather, and so on. They rarely indicate which side of the family the person is from.

Answer the following sentences with T (true) or F (false).

1. Korean words often show if the person is from the mother's or father's family.  
2. There are two words in Korean for "aunt."
3. There are no words in English that indicate if a relative is from the mother's or father's family.

A **Choose the statement which best describes what you see in the picture.** Track 11

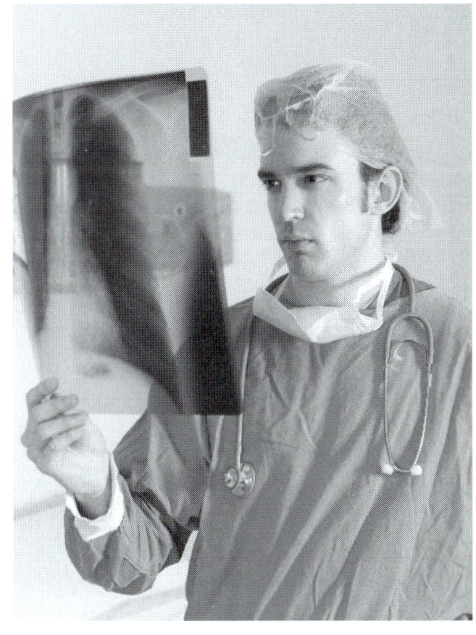

(A)　　　　　(B)　　　　　(C)　　　　　(D)

B **Listen to the question and choose the best answer.** Track 12

1. (A)　　　(B)　　　(C)
2. (A)　　　(B)　　　(C)
3. (A)　　　(B)　　　(C)

C **Choose the best answer to each question after listening to the conversation.** Track 13

4. How many people are there in her family?

   (A) Four　　　　　　　　　　　　　　　(B) Five
   (C) Six　　　　　　　　　　　　　　　　(D) Seven

5. Which statement is true?

   (A) The woman is the oldest child.　　　　(B) Her mother is a banker.
   (C) The woman has two older sisters and a brother.　　(D) Her eldest sibling is a sister.

03 My House

Vocabulary

living room	dining room	chores	rug	lamp
furniture	vacuum	wipe	appliances	placed

Complete the sentences with vocabulary words.

1. Every evening, our family sits in the ________________ and watches TV.
   우리 가족은 매일 저녁 거실에 앉아 TV를 본다.

2. My father is using a sponge to ________________ the bench clean.
   아버지가 스펀지를 사용하여 벤치를 닦고 있다.

3. Parents and teenagers often argue about small matters such as clothes, homework, phone use, and household ________________.
   부모들과 십대들은 대개 옷, 숙제, 전화사용이나 집안일 같은 사소한 일로 다툰다.

4. The price includes both the house and the ________________ inside of it.
   그 가격에는 집과 그 안에 있는 가구가 포함되어 있다.

5. A washing machine is one of the most convenient home ________________.
   세탁기는 가장 편리한 가전용품 중 하나이다.

6. It goes with the ________________ on the floor, but I don't think it matches the couch.
   그것은 바닥의 양탄자와는 어울리는데 소파하고는 어울리지 않는 것 같다.

7. I heard a ________________ cleaner whirring.
   진공청소기가 왱왱 돌아가는 소리를 들었다.

8. I need a desk ________________ that gives off a lot of light.
   아주 밝은 책상용 스탠드가 필요합니다.

9. Dinner's ready, so let's go to the ________________.
   저녁식사가 준비됐으니 식당으로 가시지요.

10. He ________________ his chair next to mine.
    그는 자기 의자를 내 의자 옆에 놓았다.

Ⓐ Complete the diagram with the correct names of the rooms.

1. ______________   2. ______________

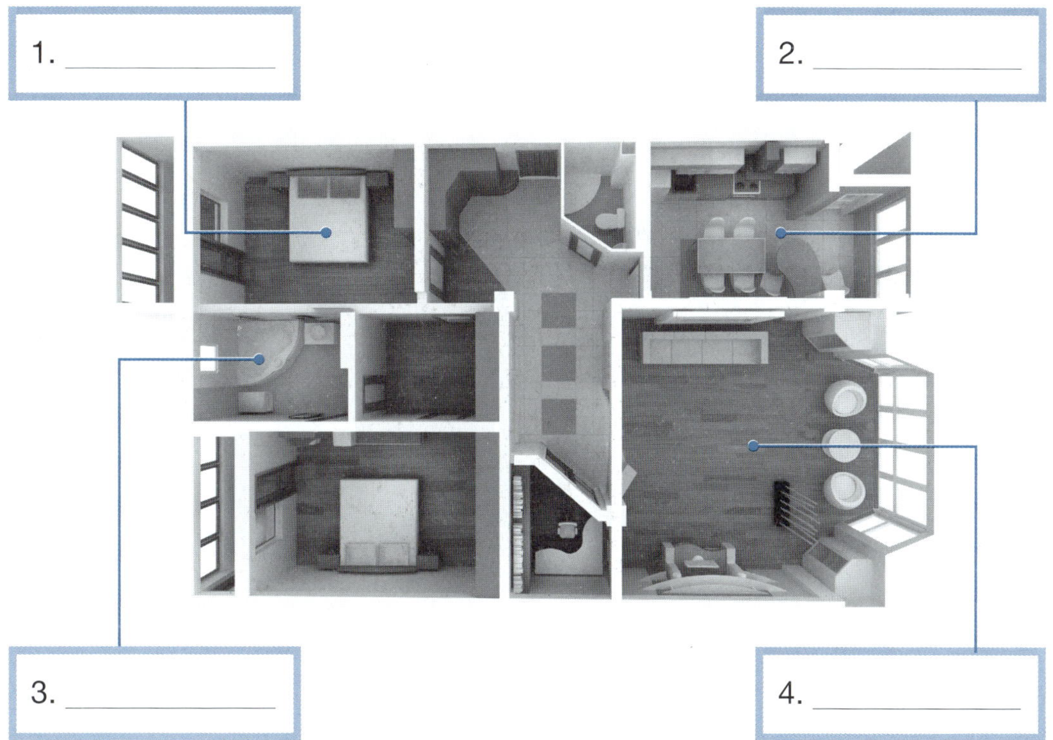

3. ______________   4. ______________

Ⓑ Complete the table.

bed	sink	toilet	sofa
rug	microwave	armchair	bookcase
closet	bathtub	blender	towel
refrigerator	pillow	dresser	toothpaste

Living room	Kitchen	Bedroom	Bathroom

A   **Look at the picture. Then use the words to fill in the blanks.**

| between | next to | on | behind | under | in front of |

1. The books are ________________ Emily's desk.
2. The keyboard is ________________ the monitor.
3. The bag is ________________ the two desks.
4. The trash can is ________________ Tom's desk.
5. The umbrella is ________________ Emily's desk.
6. Tom is standing ________________ his desk.

B   **Listen to the conversation and complete the picture.**   Track 14

C Complete the sentences with appropriate words.

To tidy a messy room, I …

1. c_____________ the window.
2. m_____________ the bed.
3. w_____________ the desk.
4. v_____________ the rug.
5. m_____________ the floor.

D Listen to the conversation and match the items with the places. Track 15

1. watch   a. in the bag
2. book   b. next to the TV
3. cell phone   c. in the book
4. wallet   d. on the table
5. bag   e. under the table
6. money   f. on the TV

E Make a drawing according to the following sentences.

A secretary is sitting behind a desk. There's a light above the desk.
There's a laptop computer on the desk. There are some pens to the right of the computer. The pens are between the telephone and the computer.
There's a trash can under the desk. There's a briefcase next to the desk.

Reading

Read the passage.

When I was young, my favorite place was my home. Our house had a yard with some trees and flowers. My family had a dog named Joy. I used to play hide-and-seek with Joy. When I ran, she followed me.

On one of the trees, there was a tire hanging from a rope. My brother and I used to swing on the tire. I sometimes pretended to be Tarzan, shouting loudly as I swung back and forth. My brother and I also used to climb the tree, but I fell off once and hurt myself. After that, we didn't do any more tree climbing.

I lived in that house until I was 15 years old. I still remember my childhood home now. It was like an amusement park and an outdoor laboratory to learn about nature all in one. I really liked that house. I hope to have a similar house for my own family in the future.

Answer the following sentences with T (true) or F (false).

1. There were few trees and flowers around the house. T F
2. His family moved when he was 15 years old. T F
3. He went to an amusement park and a laboratory when he was young. T F

A   **Choose the statement which best describes what you see in the picture.** 🔊 Track 16

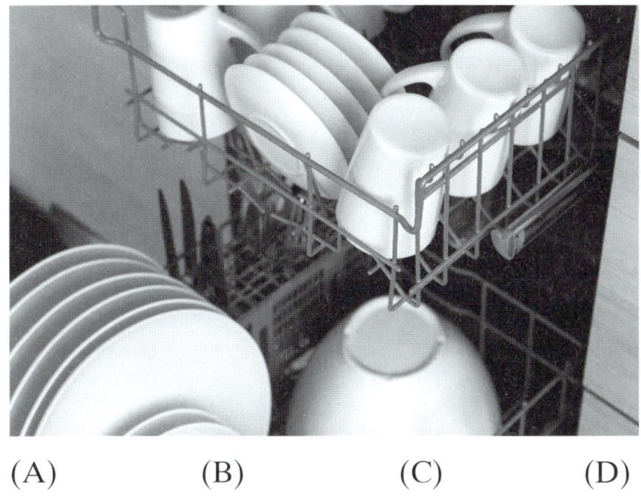

(A)   (B)   (C)   (D)

B   **Listen to the question and choose the best answer.** 🔊 Track 17

1. (A)   (B)   (C)
2. (A)   (B)   (C)
3. (A)   (B)   (C)

C   **Choose the best answer to each question after listening to the conversation.** 🔊 Track 18

4. What will the woman do first?

     (A) She will clear the table.   (B) She will vacuum the floor.
     (C) She will clean the sink.   (D) She will eat lunch first.

5. Where are new trash bags?

     (A) Outside   (B) Under the sink
     (C) In the trash can   (D) On the floor

04 Numbers

Vocabulary

degrees	centigrade	temperature	Fahrenheit	multiplication
division	addition	minus	point	equals

Complete the sentences with vocabulary words.

1. The sign "+" expresses ________________.
   + 기호는 덧셈을 나타낸다.

2. Addition, subtraction, ________________, and 3. ________________ are the basic processes of arithmetic.
   덧셈, 뺄셈, 곱셈, 나눗셈은 산수의 기본 과정이다.

4. 2 plus 4 ________________ 6.
   2 더하기 4는 6이다.

5. One half and zero ________________ five are the same.
   2분의 1과 0.5는 같다.

6. 32 degrees Fahrenheit equals 0 ________________ Celsius.
   화씨 32도는 섭씨 0도이다.

7. Water freezes at 0 degrees ________________.
   물은 섭씨 0도에서 언다.

8. Overall, global temperatures have risen by 1 degrees ________________.
   전 기간을 통틀어서 지구의 기온이 화씨 1도 상승하였다.

9. The ________________ is going to be about 21 to 25 degrees tomorrow.
   내일 기온은 21도에서 25도가 될 전망입니다.

10. It's so cold! The temperature is ________________ ten degrees out there.
    정말 추워요! 바깥 온도는 영하 10도에요.

Ⓐ Complete the calendar using ordinal numbers.

Sunday	Monday				Friday	Saturday
•	First		Third			Sixth
Seventh			Tenth	Eleventh		Thirteenth
	Fifteenth	Sixteenth		Eighteenth	Nineteenth	
	Twenty second			Twenty fifth	Twenty sixth	Twenty seventh
	Twenty ninth		Thirty first	•	•	•

Ⓑ Order the months of the year using ordinal numbers.

January _____________   June _____________   December _____________

July _____________   August *Eighth*   May _____________

February _____________   April _____________   November _____________

March _____________   October _____________   September _____________

Ⓒ Complete the exercise by writing cardinal numbers and making number amounts.

1. thirteen
2. thirty-one
3. one hundred twenty four
4. 2,345
5. twelve thousand and ten
6. 711,300
7. twelve million
8. 3,123,489
9. forty million six hundred thousand and one

A Match the numbers.

1. point five
2. zero point one
3. one point two five
4. two point oh five
5. thirteen point one five

a. 13.15
b. 0.1
c. 2.05
d. 0.5
e. 1.25

B Write the dates.

1. When is Christmas? *It's December twenty-fifth* .
2. When is Valentine's Day? ___________________________ .
3. Today is ___________________ ___________________ , ___________________ .
4. My birthday is ___________________ ___________________ , ___________________ .
5. My best friend's birthday is ___________________ ___________________ , ___________________ .

C Complete the exercise by making number amounts and writing the numbers.

1. a half   ____
2. one fourth (a quarter)   ____
3. two and three fifths   ____
4. 2/5   ____
5. 25 2/7   ____

D Fill in the blanks in the following sentences.

1. Add five and four and the sum is ___________________ .
2. Multiply the sum of 5 and 3 and sum of 4 and 6 → (5+3)x(4+6) = ___________________ .
3. Tom had three books. Teacher asked him to bring seven books. How many books does she have to buy? ___________________ books.
4. Heidi had 6 apples. She ate 3 of them. How many did she have left? ___________________ apples.
5. Seven alligators, three of them sad, the rest happy. How many happy alligators are there? ___________________ .

E **Listen and write the numbers.** Track 19

1. __________	2. __________	3. __________
4. __________	5. __________	6. __________

F **Listen and fill in the blanks with the numbers.** Track 20

1.

Place: Red tea

__________ South

Ronald Street

Time: 6:00 p.m.

2.

Mike's cell phone

____

3.

~~213 Rain Street~~

__________ Street

Read the passage.

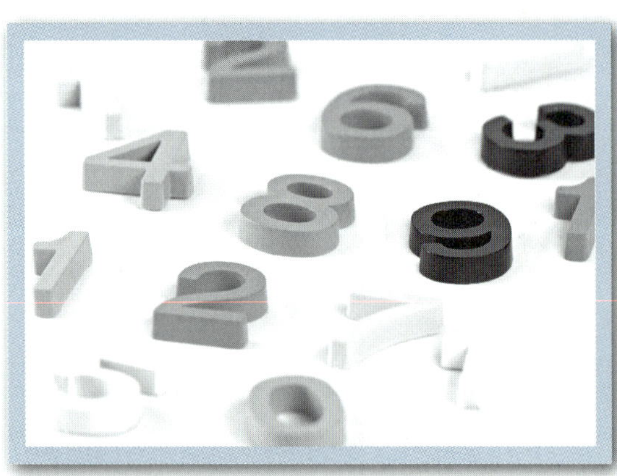

Numbers are important in every language. You need numbers for shopping, counting, telling the time, and other activities. But Koreans can be confused with numbers in English.

Take 9876543210 for example. It's a big number. Let's make it smaller. First, you should insert commas. From the right, count every three numbers, and insert a comma. Now the number should look like this: 9,876,543,210.

The next thing to do is to look ONLY at the numbers between the commas. Ignore the other numbers. Let's see what happens now: 9   876   543   210

Those numbers look simple, don't they? At the end of each series of numbers, you need to add a word. Like this: 9 billion   876 million   543 thousand   2 hundred and 10

That's all. You may think counting numbers in English is easier than in Korean! Let's read some big numbers in English now:

14,000	fourteen thousand
4,500,200	four million, five hundred thousand, two hundred
700,000,000	seven hundred million
123,456,789	one hundred twenty three million, four hundred fifty six thousand, seven hundred eighty nine

 **Answer the following sentences with T (true) or F (false).**

1. You should use commas with every three numbers.　　T　　F
2. One billion is a smaller number than million.　　T　　F
3. 20,000 is "two hundred thousand" in English.　　T　　F

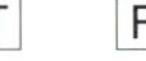

Ⓐ **Choose the statement which best describes what you see in the picture.** 🔊 Track 21

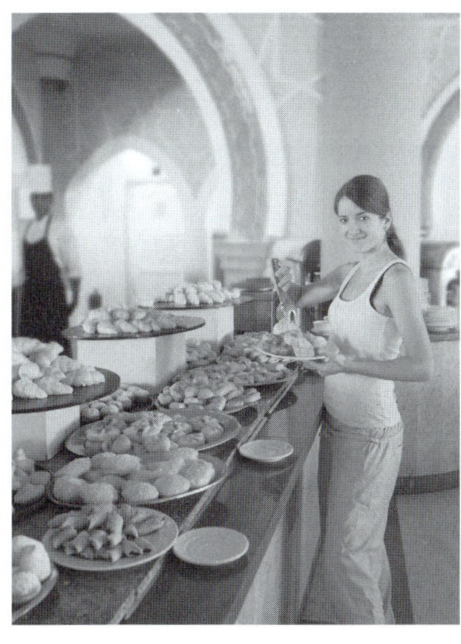

(A)   (B)   (C)   (D)

Ⓑ **Listen to the question and choose the best answer.** 🔊 Track 22

1. (A) (B) (C)
2. (A) (B) (C)
3. (A) (B) (C)

Ⓒ **Choose the best answer to each question after listening to the conversation.** 🔊 Track 23

4. Why is the man calling?

 (A) He wants to make an appointment.
 (B) He wants to leave the message for an airline employee.
 (C) He wants to reserve a flight.

5. Which statement is true?

 (A) He will depart from New York.
 (B) The flight number is 754.
 (C) East Asia Airlines has some seats on October 22nd.

05 My Schedule

Vocabulary

schedule	seldom	wake-up	arrived	go to bed
breakfast	brunch	lunch	dinner	hand

Complete the sentences with vocabulary words.

1. The hour _________________ of the clock is pointing at five.
   시계 바늘이 5시를 가리키고 있다.

2. When he _________________ at the station, he found his train had already left.
   역에 도착했을 때 그는 열차가 이미 떠나버린 것을 알았다.

3. I'm on my way out to have _________________. Will you join me?
   지금 점심식사하러 나가는 길인데 같이 갈래요?

4. I jog every morning before _________________.
   나는 매일 아침 조반 전에 조깅한다.

5. How about going out for _________________ and to see an opera tonight?
   오늘 밤 외식하고 오페라 한 편 볼까요?

6. She _________________ scolds her children for small things.
   그녀는 여간해서는 아이들을 꾸짖지 않는다.

7. As always, _________________ will be served in Meeting Room C at 10:30 a.m.
   관례대로 아침 겸 점심은 10시 반에 C 회의실에서 제공됩니다.

8. I would like to receive a _________________ call in the morning.
   아침에 모닝콜을 받으면 좋겠습니다.

9. Let me tell you about my daily _________________.
   제 하루 일과에 대해서 말씀 드리겠습니다.

10. She will _________________ early tonight.
    그녀는 오늘 밤 일찍 취침에 들 것이다.

Ⓐ Look at the times and match them to the correct clock faces.

a.   b.   c.   d.   e.   f.

1. eight o'clock / eight in the morning / eight a.m. _______________
2. twelve o'clock / noon / midnight _______________
3. ten fifteen / fifteen after ten / a quarter past ten _______________
4. nine forty-five / a quarter to ten / nine forty-five at night _______________
5. one thirty / half past one / one thirty p.m. _______________
6. eleven oh-five / five after eleven / five past eleven _______________

Ⓑ Fill in the blanks and look at the different ways to say the time.

1.   2.   3.   4.

1. It's _______________ o'clock.
2. It's _______________ fifteen. / It's a quarter after _______________ .
3. It's _______________ thirty. / It's half past _______________ .
4. It's _______________ forty-five. / It's a quarter to _______________ .

Ⓒ Fill in the blanks with the following frequency adverbs.

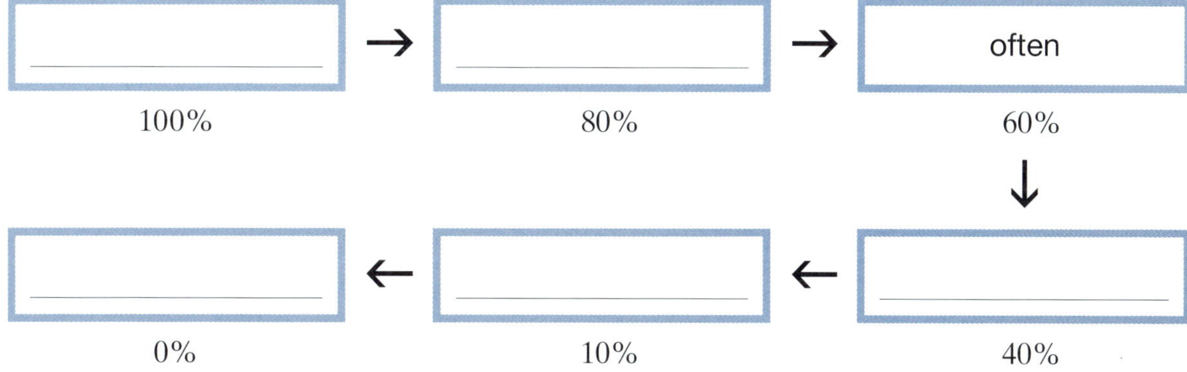

A Listen and draw the correct positions of the hands on the clocks. Track 24

1. __________ 2. __________ 3. __________ 4. __________ 5. __________

B Listen to the recording and check the time you hear. Track 25

1. a. 6:05   b. 6:15   c. 6:50
2. a. 10:05   b. 5:10   c. 5:05
3. a. 12:20   b. 12:12   c. 12:02
4. a. 3:30   b. 3:33   c. 3:03
5. a. 1:10   b. 1:50   c. 12:59

C Answer the questions.

1. What time do you get up?
2. What time do you have breakfast?
3. What time do you go to school?
4. When do you have dinner?
5. When do you go to bed?

D Answer the question with the following pictures.

  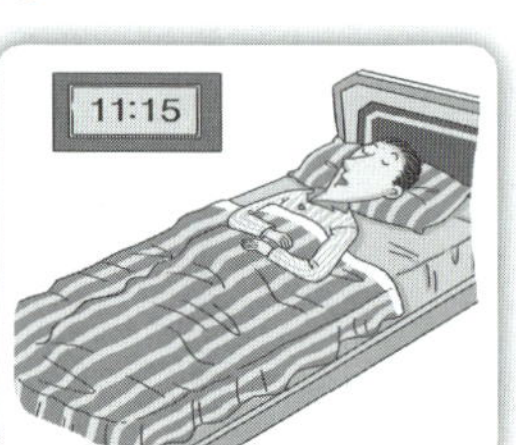

1. What does he do at 9:55 a.m.?
2. What does she do at 8:30 a.m.?
3. What does he do at 11:15?

E **Check the adverbs of frequency and answer the questions.**

Do you	always	usually	sometimes	hardly	never
1. Have breakfast?					
2. Exercise every day?					
3. Drink alcohol at least once a week?					
4. Have more than two cups of coffee per day?					
5. Sleep earlier than 11:00 p.m.?					
6. Change your cell phone ringtone?					
7. Check your e-mail every evening?					

Answer the questions above with the adverbs of frequency.

1. _I always have breakfast._
2. ____
3. ____
4. ____
5. ____
6. ____
7. ____

F **Look at the following schedule and fill in the blanks with the words in the box.**

6:00	take	walk	have
go	surf	until	dressed

I usually get up at 1. _______________. Every morning, I 2. _______________ in the park for
an hour. And then I 3. _______________ a shower. I 4. _______________ breakfast at 7:30.
Next, I get 5. _______________ and go to school at 8. I have classes 6. _______________ 4:00.
Afterwards, I work in a restaurant from 5 to 8. I get home around 9:00 and I read a book or
7. _______________ the Internet before I 8. _______________ to bed around 11 p.m.

Read the passage.

How do you spend your leisure time? People associate leisure with relaxation. They imagine themselves lying by a pool or even napping. You could spend your leisure time improving your brainpower, though.

A lack of sleep is bad for your brain. Many people do not get enough sleep. This can have a negative effect on your brainpower. People who do not get enough sleep cannot concentrate as much as those who do. Exercise and laughter are other ways to boost and strengthen brainpower. Diet is also believed to be fundamental to boosting brainpower. Oily fish contains fatty acids which increase a person's level of cognitive functions. If you do not like fish, there is another food, chocolate! Chocolate contains ingredients that increase the supply of oxygen to the brain. As well as boosting brainpower, it also lowers the risk of heart disease.

Mental activity is essential, too. Regularly doing puzzles like Sudoku boosts a person's brainpower. Unfortunately for students, research shows doing homework does this just as well.

Complete the summary.

brainpower	Sleeping	exercise	activities	relax

Leisure time is a time in which to 1. _________________ and enjoy yourself. You can also boost your 2. _________________ in some relaxing ways. 3. _________________ can help increase your brainpower. People who do not get enough sleep cannot concentrate as well as those who do. People who 4. _________________ are also helping their brainpower. Laughter and diet are also important. Oily fish and chocolate are foods that can help boost brainpower. Completing mental 5. _________________ such as puzzles and crosswords puzzles can keep the human brain sharp.

A Choose the statement which best describes what you see in the picture.  Track 26

(A)   (B)   (C)   (D)

B Listen to the question and choose the best answer. Track 27

1. (A)   (B)   (C)
2. (A)   (B)   (C)
3. (A)   (B)   (C)

C Choose the best answer to each question after listening to the conversation. Track 28

4. Why does she want to delay the meeting?

(A) She feels tired.   (B) She has many things to do now.
(C) He wants to stay in her office.   (D) She wants to call him.

5. What time will they probably have their meeting?

(A) At five   (B) At six
(C) At seven   (D) At eight

06 May I try this on?

Vocabulary

browsing	checkout	change	customers	refund
clearance sale	price tag	cost	try on	expensive

Complete the sentences with vocabulary words.

1. I spent the afternoon _________________ in book stores.
   서점에서 책을 구경하며 오후를 보냈어요.

2. This Sunday we're having our biggest ever year-end _________________!
   이번 주 일요일에 사상 최대의 연말 재고품 세일을 합니다!

3. Could you please make your selections and head towards the _________________?
   물건을 고르신 다음 계산대로 와주십시오.

4. Give me my _________________ in pennies, please.
   거스름돈은 동전(페니)으로 주세요.

5. It's quite _________________ and costs a lot to maintain.
   가격이 비싸고 유지비용이 많이 들어요.

6. I cannot give you a _________________ without the receipt, I'm afraid.
   죄송하지만, 영수증 없이는 환불해드릴 수 없습니다.

7. Can I _________________ this jacket, please?
   이 재킷을 입어봐도 되나요?

8. The meal _________________s 20 dollars per head.
   식사는 한 사람당 20달러이다.

9. This shop offers delivery service for approved _________________.
   우리 가게는 고객들을 위해 배달 서비스를 제공합니다.

10. The clerk is scanning a _________________.
   점원이 가격표를 스캔하고 있다.

Ⓐ Look at the coins and write how much it is.

1. 
2. 
3. 
4.
5. 

penny	nickel	dime	quarter	dollar/buck
__________ ¢	__________ ¢	__________ ¢	__________ ¢	__________ ¢ / $1

Ⓑ How much is it?

1. $__________________

2. $__________________

3. __________________ ¢

Ⓒ List the following words in the correct heading.

sneakers	jeans	sandals	loafers
pants	shorts	a vest	a dress shirt
heels	a skirt	a blouse	a jacket

Tops	Bottoms	Shoes

A Look at the pictures and answer the questions.

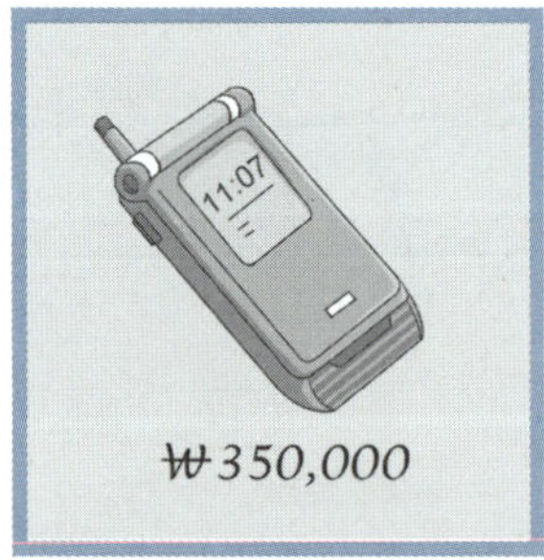

₩350,000

₩1,200,000

$150.00

$125.99

1. How much does the monitor cost? _______________________
2. How much does the cell phone cost? _______________________
3. How much does the MP3 player cost? _______________________
4. How much does the DVD player cost? _______________________

B Match the question and the proper answer.

1. May I help you?	a. I think I'm a small.
2. What size do you need?	b. Yes, but only if you have a receipt.
3. How much are they?	c. No, thank you. I'm just browsing.
4. Where's the fitting room?	d. It's on the left, next to the checkout counter.
5. Do you give refunds?	e. They are $40 each, or two for $65.

C Match the words with their definitions.

1. price	a. how much the product costs
2. quality	b. the name of the company or maker
3. brand	c. how easy/difficult it is to use a product
4. popularity	d. how much other people like the product
5. convenience	e. how well made a product is

D Listen to the conversation and check T (True) or F (False). Track 29

1. She bought the pants with a zipper. T F
2. Her mother bought the item. T F
3. She wants to exchange the pants. T F
4. The store will give her a refund on the pants. T F

E   Listen to the conversation, check the clothes the boy will get and make a total.

Track 30

What he will get	
Price	Total $

F   Listen and check on the right category in the chart below. Track 31

	off-line shopping	online shopping	home shopping
1.			✔
2.			
3.			
4.			
5.			
6.			

 **Read the passage.**

RE: Order Summary from gap.com
From: "Gap Online Customer Service" <custserv@gap.com>
Sent: Fri, 14 Nov 2009 11:24:18 -0500 (EST)
To: "Monica Lee" <monicalee@yahoo.co.kr>

Dear Monica,
Thank you for shopping at gap.com. Your order confirmation number is 104536074. Print out this page or record this number, in case you have any questions.
Here is a summary of your order:

ORDER #: 104536074 RECEIVED ON: 2009-11-14 11:08:00
Shipment #1 to: Monica Lee
24 Apple Ave. Fort Lee, NJ 07024

Description	Size	Color	Qty	Price
Baby Gap gift box			1	$5.00
Velvet Party Dress	2XL	scarlet	1	$26.99

(If you make a purchase at gap.com, you will receive order and shipping confirmation emails.)
If you have any questions, please email us at custserv@gap.com, or call us at 1.800.GAP. STYLE.

Thank you again for your order,
Gap.com Customer Service

Answer the questions.

1. What did Monica order?
2. If she has any questions, where should Monica call?
3. How much should Monica pay in total?

A **Choose the statement which best describes what you see in the picture.** 🔈 Track 32

(A)　　　　(B)　　　　(C)　　　　(D)

B **Listen to the question and choose the best answer.** 🔈 Track 33

1. (A)　　　(B)　　　(C)
2. (A)　　　(B)　　　(C)
3. (A)　　　(B)　　　(C)

C **Choose the best answer to each question after listening to the conversation.** 🔈 Track 34

4. Where is the cosmetics section?

   (A) In aisle 2　　　　　　　　(B) In aisle 4
   (C) In aisle 5　　　　　　　　(D) In aisle 9

5. What is the woman NOT shopping for today?

   (A) Sneakers　　　　　　　　(B) Jeans
   (C) Cosmetics　　　　　　　　(D) Heels

Would you like to order now?

Vocabulary

served	aisle	take-out	order	seafood
organic	Side dishes	medium-rare	plastic bag	dressing

Complete the sentences with vocabulary words.

1. Let's count heads so we'll know how many hamburgers to _______________.
   햄버거를 몇 개 주문할지 알 수 있게 인원 수를 세어보자.

2. What kind of _______________ would you like on your salad?
   샐러드에는 어떤 드레싱을 원하십니까?

3. Room service is _______________ in a person's hotel room, rather than the hotel restaurant.
   룸서비스는 호텔 레스토랑보다는 개인의 호텔 룸에서 제공된다.

4. _______________ come with a main course in many Korean meals.
   많은 한국 음식들은 주요리에 반찬들이 곁들어진다.

5. A _______________ steak has pink, slightly cooked meat in its center.
   미디엄–레어 스테이크는 선분홍색을 띠고 고기 가운데가 살짝 익혀진 것이다.

6. Many people believe that _______________ foods are safe due to their lack of chemicals.
   많은 사람들은 유기농 식품은 화학성분이 적기 때문에 안전하다고 믿는다.

7. I will try not to use _______________ so I can help the environment.
   나는 환경을 위해 비닐 봉지를 사용하지 않을 것이다.

8. Most fast food places serve _______________ food as well as having an eat-in option.
   대부분의 패스트푸드 식당들은 테이블 서비스뿐만 아니라 포장 서비스(테이크 아웃)도 제공한다.

9. The _______________ spaghetti was delicious and the salad was very fresh.
   해산물 스파게티가 맛있었고 샐러드는 아주 신선했어요.

10. The dairy products are in the fridge in _______________ six.
    유제품은 6번 통로 냉장고에 있습니다.

A **Complete the table.**

shrimp	crab	salmon	cheese
butter	eggplant	sweet potato	milk
lobster	vinegar	cabbage	carrot
cream	oyster	salt	soy sauce

Dairy section	Seafood	Condiments	Produce section

B **Listen and circle the woman's food in red and the man's food in black.** Track 35

A **Look at the menu. With a partner, imagine you are a customer in a restaurant and your partner is a waiter. Take turns to order food from each other.**

Appetizers	☐ French fries	☐ Onion rings	☐ Mozzarella sticks
	☐ Potato skins	☐ Garlic bread tower	
Main dishes	☐ T-bone steak	☐ New York strip steak ☐ Sirloin steak	
	☐ Salmon steak	☐ Steak and shrimp combo	
Side dishes	☐ Potato (mashed, boiled, baked)		☐ Sweet potato
	☐ Steamed vegetables		
	☐ Salad (potato, garden, coleslaw)		
Drinks	☐ Tea ☐ Coffee ☐ Coke ☐ Sprite ☐ Lemonade		
Desserts	☐ Cheese cake	☐ Ice cream	☐ Apple pie

B **Match the following.**

1. Will that be for here or to go?
2. How would you like your steak?
3. Can you refill the water jug, please?
4. I'd like to order a pizza to be delivered.
5. I'd like a chicken sandwich combo.
6. May I get you something to drink?

a. For here, please.
b. Sure, I'll be right back.
c. Just water, please.
d. Medium well-done, please.
e. What kind of pizza would you like?
f. Okay. The total is $7.50.

C **Complete the sentences about eating in a fast food restaurant.**

tray	turn	leftovers	trash can	lid

1. Stand in line and wait your _______________.
2. Order a hamburger, fries and a drink.
3. Put them on a _______________.
4. Take your straw and put it through the _______________ of your soda cup.
5. Enjoy eating your hamburger and fries.
6. Put the _______________ of your meal in the _______________.

D **Complete the sentences with the following words.**

checkout	aisle	plastic bag	free	dairy	frozen	basket

Shopping for Groceries

Tom gets a shopping cart.

Some people use a small plastic shopping ________________ instead of a cart.

He checks his shopping list.

In the fresh produce section, he checks the fruit and vegetables.

He puts some fruit in a ________________ .

Next, he picks up some fresh meat at the meat counter.

He goes through the canned-goods ________________ .

He gets some milk in the ________________ section.

He tries a ________________ sample of some pizza.

Tom gets a ________________ pizza from the large freezer.

Finally, he goes to the ________________ counter.

E **Match the following recipe with the correct picture.**

1. 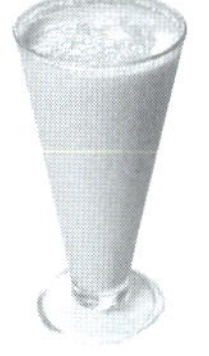

a. First, put ice cream in a blender. Next, add milk and flavoring syrup. Then, turn on the blender for one minute. Finally, pour it into a big glass, and enjoy!

2. 

b. Combine the chicken, celery, mayonnaise, onion and pickle and mix well. Season with the garlic powder, salt and pepper. Serve it on fresh crusty bread roll or bun.

3. 

c. Put a tomato in boiling water for 20 seconds and peel it. Put the tomato in a blender. Next add some milk, walnuts and honey. Then turn on the blender. It's very good for your health!

Read the passage.

The effects of fast food on the health of the average American have been a controversial issue for years. In February 2003, a thirty-two-year-old documentary maker called Morgan Spurlock decided to test the effects of fast food on his body. He only ate fast food purchased from the same world-famous burger chain. He ate there three times a day, consuming an average of 5,000 calories per day. Every time he was offered the supersize option to maximize the portion size, he had to say yes.

Spurlock was 188 centimeters tall and weighed 84 kilograms when the experiment began. After just five days of only eating fast food, he had gained 4.5 kilograms. The documentary shows him vomiting up a lunchtime supersize burger meal in the restaurant car park. He develops depression as well as headaches and fatigue. The only cure for these, he finds, is

another meal from the same restaurant. After experiencing liver damage, a doctor advises him to stop the experiment. At the end of the thirty days, his weight is 95.5 kilos. He has eaten more fast food in a month than the average American should eat in 8 years.

The film *Super Size Me!* was nominated for an Oscar, yet some people criticized the filmmaker's methodology. It was suggested that he had a preexisting liver weakness. He was criticized for overeating. Also, it was said, the average fast food customer does not live on a diet of burgers and fries alone. Others questioned why Spurlock chose not to do any exercise during the period of the experiment. Nevertheless, the film raised the level of debate about the health effects of fast food on health. A telling fact was that two months after the film premiered, the world-famous burger chain removed the supersize option from its menus.

Complete the sentences using the words provided.

effects	criticized	gained	supersize	depression

1. A documentary maker tested the ________________ of fast food on his body.
2. He would always ________________ his meals when asked to.
3. He developed ________________, headaches, and fatigue.
4. He ________________ over 11 kilograms in one month.
5. The film was nominated for an Oscar, but was also ________________.

Ⓐ Choose the statement which best describes what you see in the picture. 🔊 Track 36

(A)   (B)   (C)   (D)

Ⓑ Listen to the question and choose the best answer. 🔊 Track 37

1. (A)   (B)   (C)
2. (A)   (B)   (C)
3. (A)   (B)   (C)

Ⓒ Choose the best answer to each question after listening to the conversation. 🔊 Track 38

4. Where does this conversation take place?

(A) Steak house   (B) Fast food restaurant
(C) Bank   (D) Cafeteria

5. Which statement is true?

(A) The man ordered medium sized steak.
(B) The man wanted to eat at home.
(C) He ordered lemonade.
(D) He ordered the Bulgogi burger set menu and extra French fries.

08 Where am I?

 Vocabulary

direction	stationery	bakery	pharmacy	theater
turn left	intersection	cross	map	Go straight

Complete the sentences with vocabulary words.

1. _________________ and you will see the convenience store on your right.
   직진하면 우측에 편의점이 보일 거예요.

2. He walked away in the opposite _______________.
   그는 반대 방향으로 걸어갔다.

3. Could you tell me how to find the nearest _______________?
   가장 가까운 약국이 어디 있는지 좀 가르쳐 주시겠습니까?

4. Let's _______________ the street at the crosswalk.
   건널목에서 길을 건너자.

5. Go straight for one block and then _______________.
   한 블록 직진 후에 좌회전하세요.

6. You mean the _______________ across from the gas station?
   주유소 맞은 편에 위치한 극장 말씀하시는 건가요?

7. Can you show us where we are on the _______________, please?
   지도에서 우리가 어디 있는지 가르쳐 줄래요?

8. Danny stopped his car at the _______________ when he saw the lights turn red.
   Danny는 빨간 불로 바뀐 것을 보고 교차로에서 차를 멈추었다.

9. She needed a pen so she went to the _______________ store to buy one.
   그녀는 펜이 필요해서 그것을 사러 문구점에 갔다.

10. The bookstore is just next to the _______________.
   서점은 제과점 바로 옆에 있어요.

A **Match the directions and the pictures.**

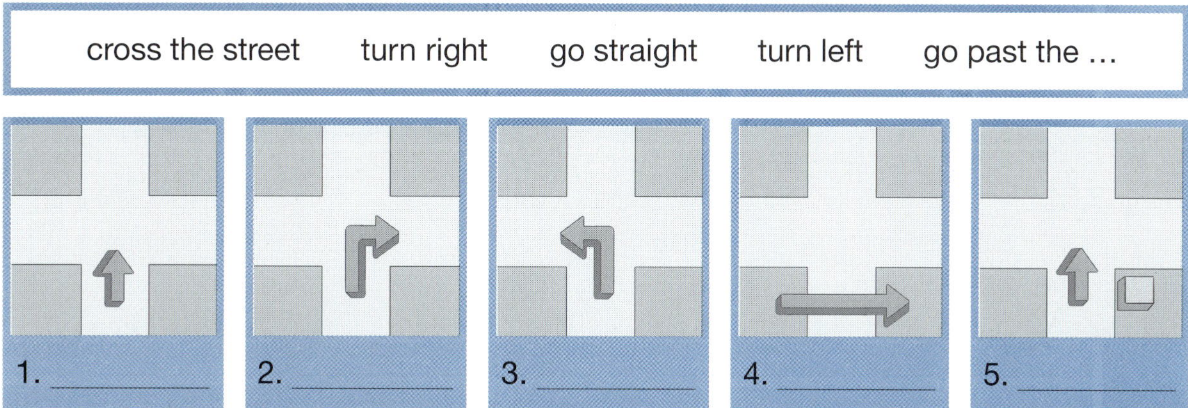

B **Look at the map. Complete the sentences with the following words.**

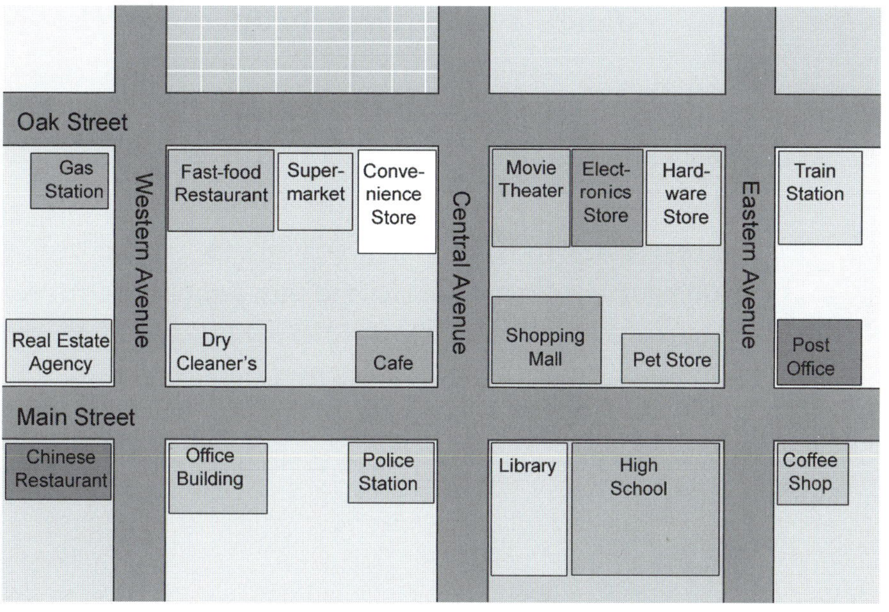

between   across from   next to

1. The convenience store is __________________ the supermarket.
2. The electronics store is __________________ the Movie Theater and hardware store.
3. The post office is __________________ the coffee shop.

A Match the place with the description.

1. A building where bread, pastries, and cakes are baked, or a shop where they are sold
2. A shop or a department in a shop where medicines are sold or given out
3. A place where you can buy fuel for your car
4. A building where you can buy stamps and use postal services
5. A building where fire fighters wait until they are called to put out fire

a. fire station

b. bakery

c. post office
d. pharmacy

e. gas station

B Read the invitation and circle Jane's house.

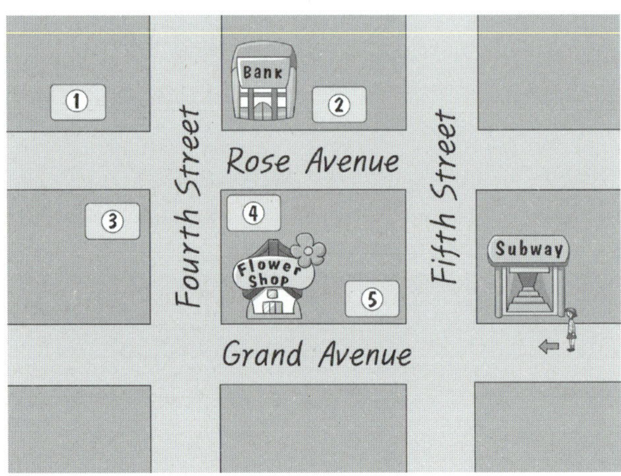

Jane's Twenty First Birthday Party!

I will be 21 on January 7, 2010.
Please join me to celebrate from 7:00 p.m.

Getting to my house

Take subway Line 4 to Hillside station. Use exit 1 and cross Fifth Street.
Go straight down Grand Avenue and turn right on the corner where
there is a flower shop. Go down one block and turn right.
You'll find my house next to the bank.
R.S.V.P. to Jane
010-823-1234

C   **Listen to the directions and complete the exercise.** (Track 39)

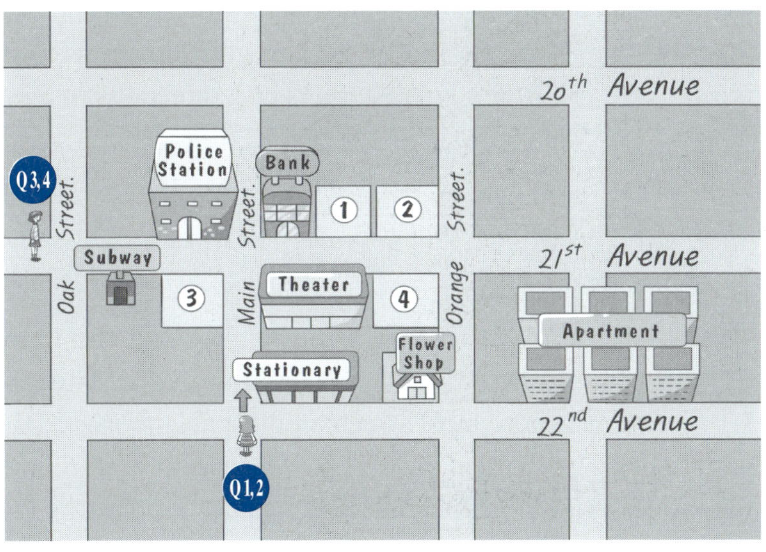

1. _________________

2. _____Post office_____

3. _________________

4. _________________

D   **Listen and follow the directions. Where do you get to?** (Track 40)

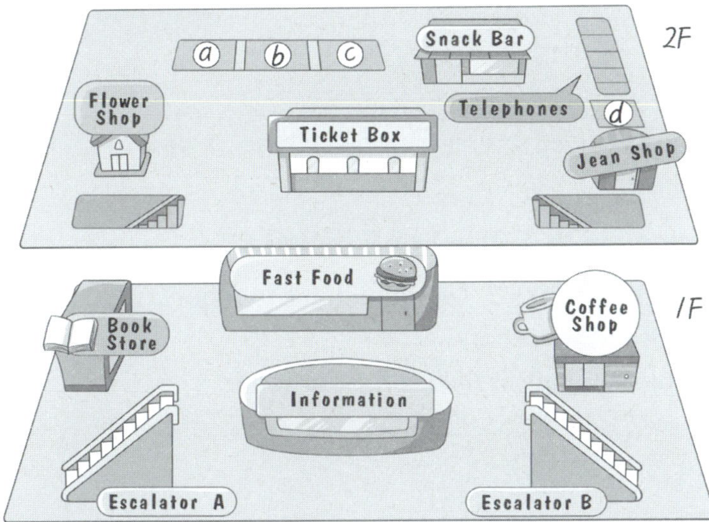

1. _________________

2. _________________

 **Read the passage.**

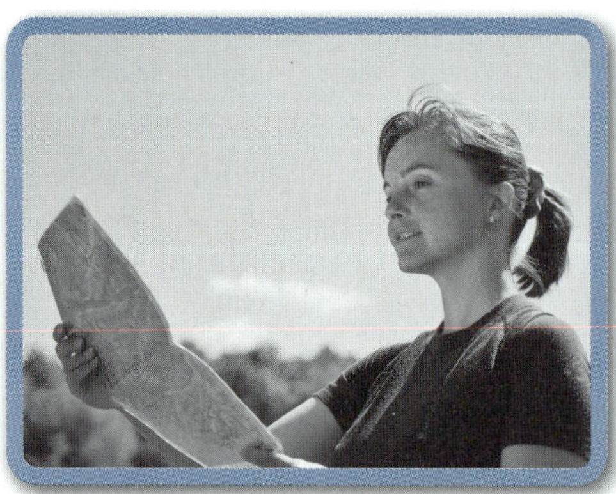

Koreans and Westerners give directions to places differently. Westerners give directions to a person like this:

Go straight down Robinson Street, and then turn left onto Third Avenue. You'll see the gas station on the corner of Elm Street and Third Avenue.

To Westerners, street names and the numbers of buildings are very important. They know where most streets in their neighborhood are, so they can find places using addresses. The Korean style, however, is quite different. Most Koreans do NOT know the names of streets. Instead, Koreans use landmarks to give directions. So Koreans might give directions like this:

I'll meet you in front of the Bodyshop across the street from the Kyobo Building.
I live in Dong Ah Apartments. They're behind Exit 5 at Shindorim Station.

This system can be difficult to foreigners, especially for apartment names. Many apartments in Korea have similar names. So, give specific directions to foreigners, or they might get lost!

 **Answer the following sentences with T (true) or F (false).**

1. Koreans often mention landmarks when they give directions to others. T F
2. Street names are very important to Westerners. T F
3. All Koreans know the names of the roads in their neighborhood. T F

Ⓐ Choose the statement which best describes what you see in the picture. 🔊 Track 41

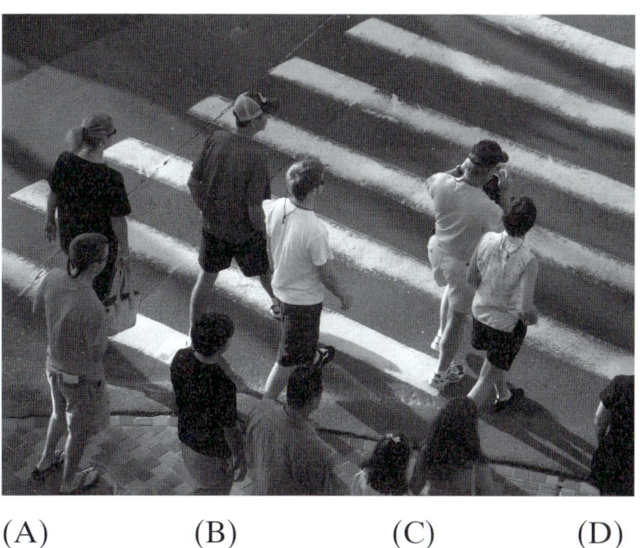

(A)　　　　(B)　　　　(C)　　　　(D)

Ⓑ Listen to the question and choose the best answer. 🔊 Track 42

1. (A)　　　(B)　　　(C)
2. (A)　　　(B)　　　(C)
3. (A)　　　(B)　　　(C)

Ⓒ Choose the best answer to each question after listening to the conversation. 🔊 Track 43

4. Where should the man start from?

    (A) UK University subway station　　　　(B) A book store
    (C) Star Apartments　　　　(D) The Star building

5. Which statement is true?

    (A) The man should take the bus number 1.
    (B) The woman lives in an apartment next to the book store.
    (C) The man should transfer to subway line 1.
    (D) The woman lives close to a university.

09 My spare time

 Vocabulary

box-office	released	director	screenplays	preview
rated	soundtrack	hobby	rerun	Advance tickets

Complete the sentences with vocabulary words.

1. His new album was recently _________________.
   그의 새로운 앨범이 최근에 발매되었다.

2. Her _______________ is watching movies.
   그녀의 취미는 영화를 보는 것이다.

3. We invite you to attend a special _______________ of our newest film.
   여러분을 저희 최신작 특별 시사회에 초대합니다.

4. Miller spent almost 70 years writing plays, _______________, novels, and essays.
   Miller는 거의 70년간 희곡, 영화 대본, 소설, 수필 등을 집필하며 살았습니다.

5. The movie was a huge _______________ success.
   그 영화는 막대한 흥행성적을 올렸다.

6. Both movies are _______________ PG.
   두 영화 모두 부모 동반 관람가 등급입니다.

7. I visited the website for the movie and bought the _______________.
   나는 그 영화와 관련된 웹사이트를 방문해서 영화음악을 구입했다.

8. The _______________ asked me to play the part of Juliet in our production of *Romeo and Juliet*.
   감독이 내게 우리가 제작하는 〈로미오와 줄리엣〉에서 줄리엣 역을 하라고 했다.

9. _______________ are $7 for adults and $4 for students.
   예매표는 성인 7달러, 학생 4달러입니다.

10. When I checked the TV schedule for the holiday, it was all just a _______________.
    내가 휴일 TV 스케줄을 확인했을 때, 재방송밖에 안 했다.

Ⓐ Complete the table.

rating	composition	scuba diving	R&B
gospel	producer	director	screenplay
jogging	riding a bike	lyrics	soccer
prime time	soap opera	sitcom	commercial break

Music	Movie	Sports	TV

Ⓑ Match the following movies with the appropriate genre.

1. comedy
2. documentary
3. fantasy
4. science fiction
5. horror
6. animation

a. Little Mermaid
b. Harry Potter
c. Star Wars
d. Mr. Bin
e. Super Size Me
f. The Ring

Ⓒ Match the question and answer.

1. Is there anything interesting on the tube?
2. Is this concert being shown live on TV?
3. Please change the channel.
4. Tom watches five hours of TV every day.

a. He's such a couch potato.
b. There are only reruns on.
c. No, it's a delayed broadcast.
d. I don't have the remote control.

A **Match the names and meanings with the cassette player buttons.**

| Eject | Record (Rec) | Rewind (Rew) | Play |
| Fast forward (F.F) | Pause | Stop | |

1. _______________ 
2. _______________ 
3. _______________ 
4. _______________

5. _______________
6. _______________ 
7. _______________ 

B **Complete the sentences with the film industry terms.**

| blockbuster | new release | original soundtrack |
| PG-13 | premiere | trailer(s) |

1. I haven't seen the movie, but I've listened to the _______________ many times.
2. Rent one _______________, and get an older DVD rental free.
3. Every summer, the major movie studios release many _______________ movies.
4. The term "_______________" comes from their having originally been shown at the end of a film program, however, _______________ are now shown before the film begins.
5. _______________ movies have material which may be inappropriate for children under 13, such as violence, bad language, and adult scenes.
6. The _______________ of his new movie attracted many fans eager to see his latest work.

C **Look at the movie poster and complete the tables.**

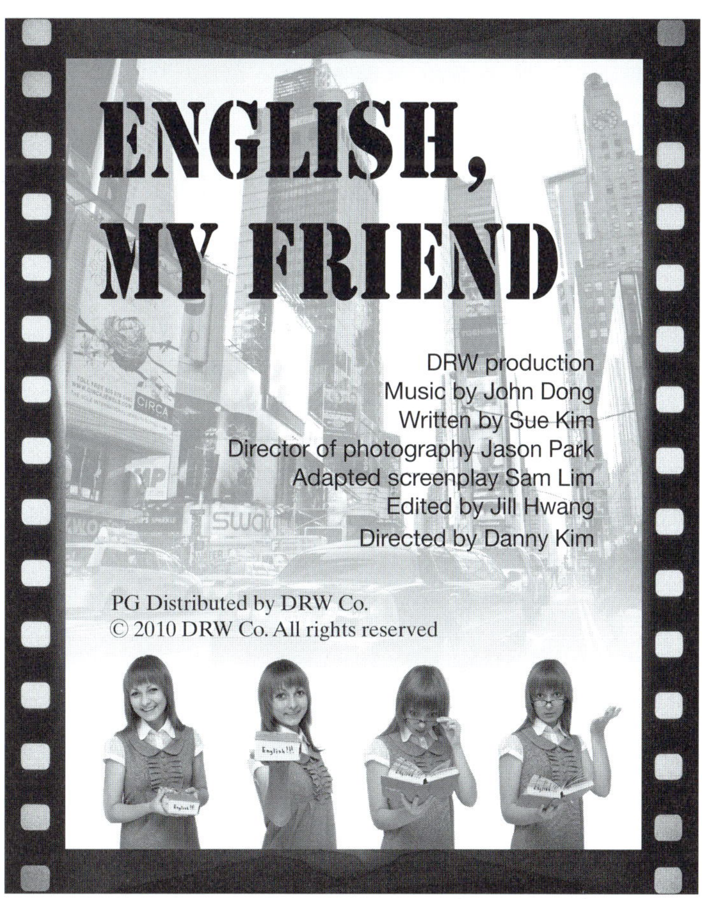

	이름
감독	
음악	
제작사	DRW
촬영감독	
시나리오 각색	
편집	
작가	
영화배급사	

	Classification and Rating
G	General Audiences
	Parental Guidance
	Recommended
	Parental Guidance Strongly
	Recommended for
	children under 13
	Restricted
	No children under 17

D **Listen and mark the following sentences true or false.** Track 44

1. This film is for adults only. T F
2. *Toyland* is showing 3 times today. T F
3. We can't watch *Toyland* at 1:00 p.m. T F

Read the passage.

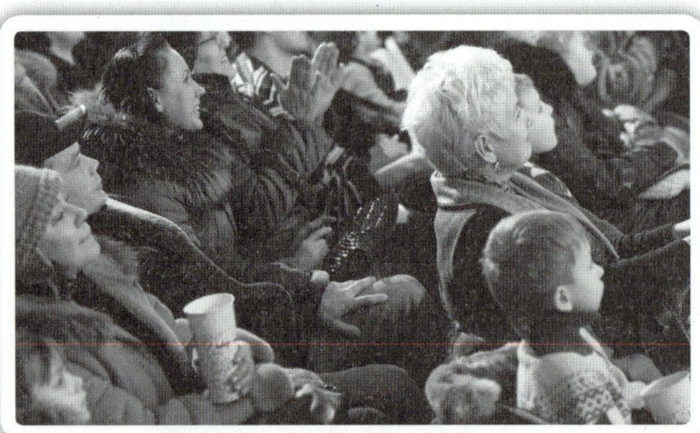

Well-dressed performers begin to play classical music on stage and the audience quietly listens. Are you worried about how to act at a classical concert? Here are good concert manners:

First, you should be on time. Once the performance starts, you cannot enter the concert hall.

Second, you should be quiet. People want to listen and feel the music. You should not do anything to distract performers, because they need to focus on their music. Don't talk or make any loud noises. No eating or taking pictures, either!

Third, you should clap at the end of the entire piece. You may be confused about when to applaud. In classical music, one piece may have several parts, each with its own ending. Clapping after each part is not polite.

Answer the questions.

1. Have you ever been to a concert? _______________________________
2. What kind of clothes would/do you wear for a concert? _______________________________

Complete the chart.

Good Manners at a Classical Concert
Be _______________________________
Sit _______________________________
Applaud _______________________________

A   **Choose the statement which best describes what you see in the picture.** Track 45

(A)   (B)   (C)   (D)

B   **Listen to the question and choose the best answer.** Track 46

1. (A)   (B)   (C)
2. (A)   (B)   (C)
3. (A)   (B)   (C)

C   **Choose the best answer to each question after listening to the conversation.**  Track 47

4. What sport does the woman's favorite player compete in?

    (A) Basketball   (B) Baseball
    (C) Soccer   (D) Swimming

5. Which statement is true?

    (A) They are playing baseball.
    (B) They are watching TV.
    (C) Her favorite player is not a good player at all.
    (D) They are reading the league record.

10 My party

Vocabulary

Halloween	Easter	Thanksgiving	costume	carol
feast	celebration	holiday	decorate	Christmas

Complete the sentences with vocabulary words.

1. People often ________________ their houses with scary monsters and ghosts during Halloween.
   사람들은 핼러윈 기간에 무서운 괴물이나 유령으로 집을 장식한다.

2. A favorite ________________ activity is an egg hunt, where children search for hidden eggs.
   인기 있는 부활절 행사는 어린이들이 숨겨진 달걀들을 찾는 '달걀 찾기'이다.

3. ________________ is a day celebrated with turkey, pumpkin pie and cranberry sauce in the U.S.
   추수감사절은 미국에서 칠면조 요리, 호박파이와 크랜베리 소스를 즐기는 날이다.

4. ________________ falls on the same day every year and features gift-giving.
   크리스마스는 매년 날짜가 같고 선물을 주는 특징이 있다.

5. On ________________, some children dress up as vampires, ghosts and witches.
   핼러윈에 몇몇 아이들은 흡혈귀와 귀신, 마녀 복장을 한다.

6. A ________________ is a seasonal song that is usually played during the Christmas season.
   캐롤은 크리스마스 시즌에 많이 연주되는 시즌 특유의 노래이다.

7. Holidays, like Chuseok in Korea and Thanksgiving in the U.S. feature a ________________.
   한국의 추석과 미국의 추수감사절과 같은 명절들은 축제의 특징을 지닌다.

8. The U.S.'s bicentennial ________________ of independence from Britain was in 1976.
   1976년에 미국은 영국으로부터 독립 200주년 기념식을 가졌다.

9. Offices were closed because it was a national ________________.
   국경일이라서 사무실들이 문을 닫았다.

10. Should I wear a witch or a ghost ________________ on Halloween?
   핼러윈 때 마녀복장을 할까, 유령복장을 할까?

Ⓐ Match the word and holiday with each picture.

1. Jack o' lantern •

• a. Christmas

2. Wreath •

• b. Easter day

3. Turkey •

• c. Thanksgiving day

4. Easter egg •

• d. Halloween

Ⓑ Complete the table.

Easter basket	Jack o' lantern	egg hunting	harvest
trick or treat	carol	reindeer	costume
Easter bunny	turkey	pumpkin pie	Santa Claus

Easter	Halloween	Thanksgiving	Christmas

Ⓐ Match the definitions.

Christmas

1. An attractive decoration you display in your home or garden
2. Large brown animals that pull Santa's sleigh
3. A circle of dried leaves and flowers
4. To go as a group from door to door singing Christmas carols
5. An abbreviation for "Christmas"

a. reindeer
b. wreath
c. ornaments
d. X-mas
e. caroling

Thanksgiving Day

1. A thickened sauce made with meat juices and flour and poured over meat and mashed potatoes
2. A traditional dessert served at Thanksgiving
3. To fill the turkey with stuffing
4. The breastbone of a turkey or chicken
5. The boat that the Pilgrims sailed on their ocean voyage to the New World

a. pumpkin pie
b. gravy
c. Mayflower
d. wishbone
e. stuff the bird

Halloween

1. A party in which people dress in silly, scary or humorous costumes
2. A small trouble-making creature resembling a small, disfigured man
3. An American Halloween custom in which children go from house to house asking for treats
4. Inhabited or visited by ghosts
5. A corpse that has been wrapped in pieces of cloth in order to preserve it

a. trick or treating
b. haunted
c. goblin
d. costume party
e. mummy

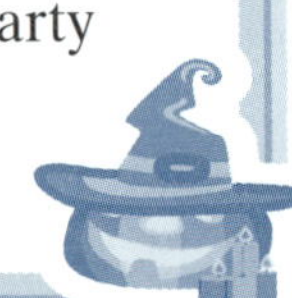

B **Complete the sentences.**

> Jack Frost
>
> white elephant
>
> get a lump of coal in your stocking
>
> trick or treat

1. A: You better behave yourself, or you're going to _________________________
   this year.
   B: You say that every year, but Santa always brings me presents.

2. A: It's absolutely freezing outside!
   B: It looks like _________________________ has been.

3. A: You never use that lamp you got for Christmas last year.
   B: It's just taking up space in my bedroom.
   It's become a real _________________________.

4. A: Okay. Harry, when they open the door, say "_________________________."
   B: Will they give me candy if I say that?

C **When are these sentences said or heard? Write C for Christmas, H for Halloween, T for Thanksgiving Day.**

1. Did you leave out milk and cookies for Santa? _________
2. I'm going to wear a witch's outfit. _________
3. We're going to carve Jack-o'-lanterns tonight. _________
4. The turkey is here! Let's say grace. _________
5. Is dad going to cook a turkey? _________

D **Match the name of party with the definition.**

> a. cocktail party
>
> d. baby shower
>
> b. housewarming party
>
> e. pajama party
>
> c. potluck party

1. A party, usually held in the early evening, where cocktails or other alcoholic _________
   drinks are served. People often dress quite formally for them.
2. An occasion when a group of young friends spend the night together at the _________
   home of one of the group. It's also called a slumber party.
3. A party that you give for friends when you have just moved to a new house. _________
4. A party that celebrate, the recent birth of a child by presenting gifts to the parents. _________
5. A party where people all bring different food. _________

 **Complete 'The Christmas Song.'**

| reindeer | Yuletide carols | mistletoe |
| spy | sleigh | Jack Frost | phrase |

The Christmas Song

Chestnuts roasting on an open fire
1. _____________ nipping at your nose
2. _____________ being sung by a choir
And folks dressed up like Eskimos

Everybody knows a turkey and some 3. _____________
Can help to make the season bright
Tiny tots, with their eyes all aglow
Will find it hard to sleep, tonight

They know that Santa's on his way
He's loading lots of toys and goodies on his 4. _____________
And every mother's child is gonna 5. _____________
To see if 6. _____________ really know how to fly...

And so I'm offering this simple 7. _____________
To kids from one to ninety-two
Although it's been said
Many times, many ways
Merry Christmas to you!

*MP3 available for teachers

Ⓐ **Choose the statement which best describes what you see in the picture.** 🔊 Track 48

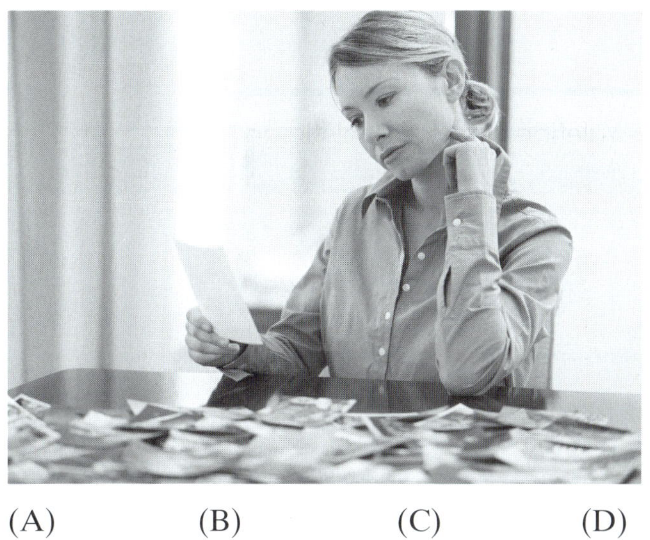

(A)   (B)   (C)   (D)

Ⓑ **Listen to the question and choose the best answer.** 🔊 Track 49

1. (A)   (B)   (C)
2. (A)   (B)   (C)
3. (A)   (B)   (C)

Ⓒ **Choose the best answer to each question after listening to the conversation.** 🔊 Track 50

4. What does the woman imply?

   (A) The man recently broke up with his girl friend.
   (B) The man is getting married soon.
   (C) The woman is having a plan to go out with the man.
   (D) The woman is not interested in his marriage.

5. Which statement is true?

   (A) The woman will meet her boyfriend on Valentine's Day.
   (B) The woman forgot the appointment to meet the man.
   (C) The woman had a wonderful time with the man.
   (D) The woman wants to marry the man.

Vocabulary

shortcuts	Wallpaper	double-click	domain	online
browser	blog	folder	attached	install

👉 Complete the sentences with vocabulary words.

1. _________________ is a large image to be used as your computer monitor's background.
   월페이퍼는 컴퓨터 모니터 배경으로 사용하는 큰 이미지이다.

2. You can import your bookmarked websites from another web _________________ or file.
   다른 웹 브라우저나 파일에서 즐겨 찾기 웹사이트를 가져올 수 있다.

3. The first step is to register a _________________ name.
   첫 번째 단계는 도메인 명을 등록하는 것이다.

4. To install your software, simply _________________ the install file and follow the instructions.
   소프트웨어를 설치하려면, 설치 파일을 더블 클릭하고 지시대로 따라하기만 하면 된다.

5. Please go to the Control Panel to _________________ system components.
   제어판으로 가서 시스템 구성요소를 설치하십시오.

6. Thanks to _________________ bookings, paper tickets are now becoming extinct.
   온라인 예약 덕분에 종이 티켓이 요즘 사라져 가고 있다.

7. She _________________ a PowerPoint file to the e-mail.
   그녀는 이메일에 파워포인트 파일을 첨부했다.

8. You can customize the name of your desktop _________________ folder.
   바탕화면의 바로가기 폴더명을 당신이 원하는 대로 지정할 수 있다.

9. Many people get their news from newspaper websites, _________________s and other electronic outlets.
   많은 사람들이 신문 웹사이트, 블로그 그리고 다른 전자매체를 통해 정보를 얻는다.

10. You can use this _________________ to store important documents.
    여러분은 중요한 자료를 보관하는데 이 폴더를 사용할 수 있습니다.

A **Translate the following e-mail terms.**

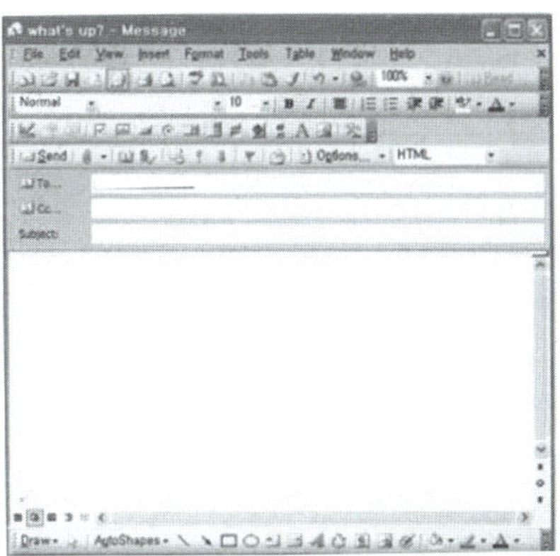

B (Bold): 볼드체	Emoticon:	To (Receiver):
Cc:	Subjects:	File: 파일
Edit:	View: 보기	e-mail account:
Drafts: 임시 보관함	Deleted:	Send:
Contact list:	Junk:	Attach:

B **Write the names of the abbreviated keyboard keys in full.**

Esc:	Alt:
Ctrl:	Del:
Ins:	F1:
Pg Up:	Pg Dn:

A **Write the appropriate Internet-related acronym.**

Company: *co.*	Korea:
Academic:	Japan:
Network:	Canada:
Military:	United Kingdom:
Organization:	France:
Government:	United States:
World Wide Web:	China:

B **Answer these questions. Circle yes or no.**

1. I have my own web page.   Yes / No
2. I often go online to communicate with friends.   Yes / No
3. I get a lot of spam in my e-mail box.   Yes / No
4. I usually do shopping for my clothes by Internet.   Yes / No
5. I use my phone to send or read text messages almost every day. Yes / No

C **Match the question with the answer.**

1. How do you start this program?   a. Double-click the icon on your desktop.
2. My computer is frozen.   b. You should install an anti-virus program.
3. I think my computer has a virus.   c. Try rebooting it.
4. Did you look at the PowerPoint attachment?   d. Yes, I printed it out.
5. What's wrong with your computer?   e. It's locked up. The cursor is frozen.

D **Look at these URLs. Read the sentences aloud using the words for the symbols.**

forward slash (/)   colon (:)   dot (.)   hyphen (-)   underscore (_)

1. www.lovestudying.co.kr/english-reading/read_the_news.htm
2. http://en.wikipedia.org/wiki/Education
3. http://www.kids-space.org/
4. http://www.foodnetwork.com/recipes-and-cooking/

E **Write the appropriate acronym.**

1. as soon as possible __________
2. by the way __________
3. date of birth __________
4. for your information __________
5. oh, I see __________
6. in my opinion __________
7. in other words __________
8. Thank God it's Friday __________
9. Oh, God! It's Monday __________
10. frequently asked questions __________

F **Match the common emoticons with their meanings.**

:O	:)	:-X	:(

1. happiness __________
2. unhappiness __________
3. surprise or screaming __________
4. my lips are sealed __________

G **Create your own Giggle Account.**

If you already have a Giggle Account, you can sign in here.

Required information for Giggle account

Your current e-mail address: __________________

e.g. myname@example.com
This will be used to sign-in to your account.

Choose a password: ________________
Re-enter password: ________________

Word Verification: Type the characters you see in the picture below.

chegrand ________________

Letters are not case-sensitive.

By clicking on "I accept" below you are agreeing to the Terms of Service above and the Privacy Policy.

I accept. Create my account.

 **Read the passage.**

The first computer game was made in 1961 by Stephen Russell, a student at the Massachusetts Institute of Technology (MIT) in the US. Two tiny ships flew around a screen trying to shoot each other in a game called Spacewar! Russell did not market his game. Instead, it was used to test computers during installations. By 2005, computer games had come so far and were so addictively popular that people had died playing them.

Addiction is the "habitual repetition of excessive behavior." Addicts are unable or unwilling to stop even though they know their behavior is harmful. In South Korea, a twenty-eight-year-old man died after playing an online computer game for fifty straight hours. Police said the man had hardly eaten or slept in that time. He had recently been fired from his job because he kept missing work to play computer games. In 2007, a thirty-year-old man from Guangzhou, China, died from exhaustion after a three-day gaming session in an Internet cafe. Meanwhile, in England, a fourteen-year-old-boy needed hospital treatment for a blood clot in his leg. He had spent the entire day kneeling in front of a game console.

Computer game addiction can be as harmful as drug of alcohol addiction. Mark Griffiths, Professor of Psychology at Nottingham Trent University in the UK, says computer game addicts suffer "the same symptoms as traditional addictions." Some men have lost their jobs and families because of their computer game addictions. Games like Starcraft and World of Warcraft are called MMORPGs, or Massively Multiplayer Online Role Playing Games. More than fifteen million people are registered for such games in South Korea, close to thirty-three percent of the population. "Computer game addiction is not taken seriously yet," adds Professor Griffiths.

 **Scan the passage for the answers and underline the related sentences.**

1. When was the first computer game made?
2. For how long did the Chinese gamer who died play computer games?
3. In which country did the fourteen-year-old boy who needed hospital treatment for a blood clot live?
4. Who is Mark Griffiths?

A **Choose the statement which best describes what you see in the picture.** 🔊 Track 51

(A)   (B)   (C)   (D)

B **Listen to the question and choose the best answer.** 🔊 Track 52

1. (A)   (B)   (C)
2. (A)   (B)   (C)
3. (A)   (B)   (C)

C **Choose the best answer to each question after listening to the conversation.** 🔊 Track 53

4. Why did the computer seem to have problem?

   (A) Because of a virus.   (B) It was turned off.
   (C) The desktop computer was dirty.   (D) The computer didn't open up.

5. Which statement is true?

   (A) The computer was sent to the repair shop.
   (B) The woman has back-up disks.
   (C) The woman couldn't access the Internet.
   (D) The man broke the woman's computer.

 12 Transport

📓 Vocabulary

traffic light	gas station	parking	pedestrian	fare
tow truck	subway	lane	crosswalk	tollgate

👉 Complete the sentences with vocabulary words.

1. Watch out! You almost hit a _______________ back there.
   조심해! 뒤에 있는 보행자를 거의 칠 뻔했어.

2. The _______________ has just turned green.
   신호등이 막 녹색으로 바뀌었다.

3. Will you drop me at the _______________?
   저 건널목에서 내려 주실래요?

4. Pull in at the next _______________.
   다음 주유소에서 차를 세우세요.

5. The vacant lot next to the office was turned into a _______________ lot.
   사무실 옆 공터가 주차장으로 변해 버렸다.

6. The taxi _______________ from the airport was reasonable.
   공항에서부터 타고 온 택시 요금은 적당했다.

7. She works at the highway _______________, collecting money from drivers.
   그녀는 고속도로 톨게이트에서 운전자에게 요금을 징수하는 일을 한다.

8. The man is leaving the _______________ station.
   남자가 지하철역을 떠나고 있다.

9. You'll have to call a _______________ and get it towed to the service station.
   견인차를 불러서 정비소에 끌고 가게 해야겠다.

10. At this intersection, you can't make a left turn from any _______________.
    이 교차로에서는 어떤 차선에서도 좌회전을 할 수 없습니다.

Ⓐ Name the parts of the car.

> steering wheel   rear-view mirror   brake   horn
> ignition   windshield wiper   accelerator   seat belt

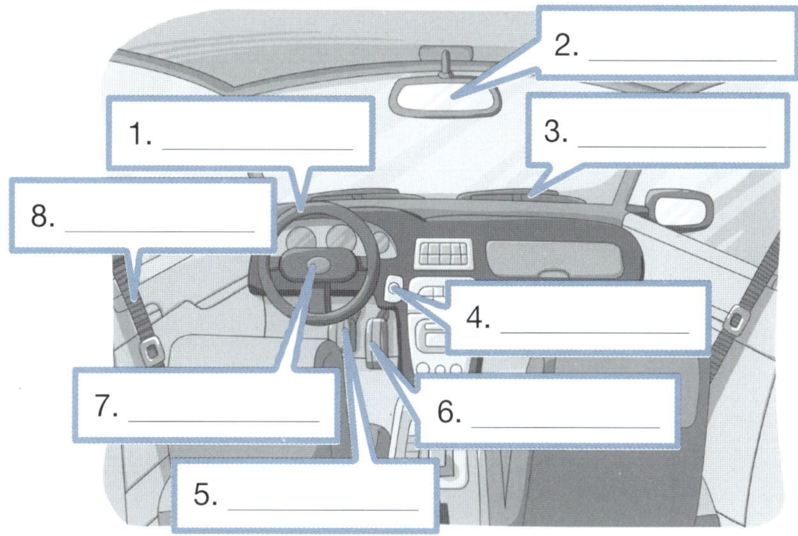

Ⓑ Match the types of vehicles with the pictures.

> a. sedan   b. limousine   c. coupe   d. convertible
> e. van   f. RV   g. pick-up truck   h. SUV

1. _________________

2. _________________

3. _________________

4. _________________

5. _________________

6. _________________

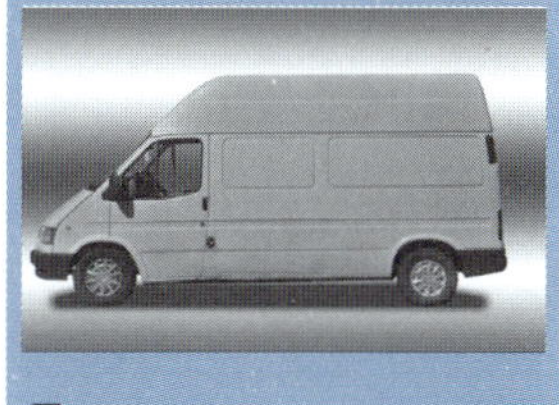

7. _________________

8. _________________

A **Complete the sentences.**

take	get off	exit	stops	flat
transfer	fare	pull over	directions	drive

1. Next stop is City Hall. You can ________________ to the red line, line number 1.
   다음 정류장은 시청입니다. 빨간색. 1호선으로 갈아타실 수 있습니다.
2. Where can I ________________ the bus? 어디에서 버스를 타나요?
3. Which stop should I ________________ the bus at? 어느 정거장에서 내려야 하나요?
4. Go out ________________ 2. 2번 출구로 나오세요.
5. How many ________________ is it from here? 여기서 몇 정거장 떨어져 있나요?
6. How much is the subway ________________? 지하철 요금이 얼마인가요?
7. Would you ________________ here, please? 여기서 세워 주시겠어요?
8. Let's stop and ask for ________________. 멈춰서 길을 물어보자.
9. It's about a 30-minute ________________ from here. 차로 여기서 약 30분 거리에요.
10. I have a ________________ tire. 제 타이어가 펑크 났어요.

B **Match the question with the answer.**

1. How often does the bus come?
2. Where is the bus stop?
3. How long is the ride?
4. How much will it cost to go downtown?
5. Am I able to park my car here?
6. You can't park here.
7. How much gas would you like?
8. The air conditioner isn't working.

a. It comes every 10 minutes.
b. It'll take about 25 minutes.
c. It's across the street.
d. $10~$20 depending on traffic.
e. I'm afraid not. This is a tow-away zone.
f. You should go to a service center, then.
g. Fill 'er up, please.
h. Why not? Is it a handicapped space?

C **Listen and number the suitable car.** Track 54

1. ________________

2. ________________

3. ________________

D Name the following traffic signs.

| a. Stop | b. No entry | c. Yield | d. Speed limitation |
| e. School zone | f. Bike lane | g. Pedestrian crossing | h. No U-turn |

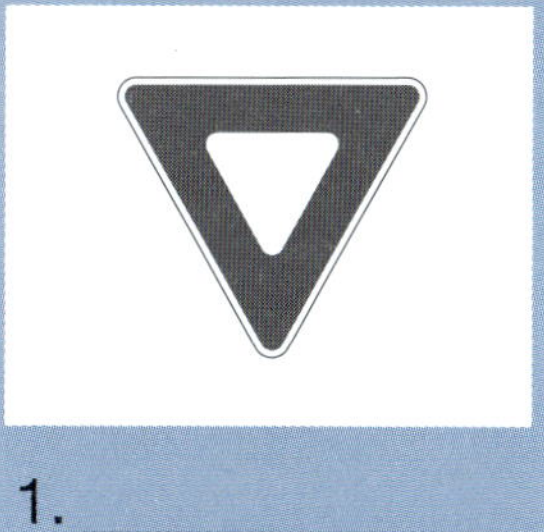 1. ___________

 2. ___________

 3. ___________

 4. ___________

 5. ___________

 6. ___________

 7. ___________

 8. ___________

E How do you go to school? Look at the sample sentences and make your own answer.

Tom	I take a bus to school every day. The bus comes every 20 minutes. I sometimes miss a bus, and if that happens, I'm late for my class.
John	I take the subway to work because I don't have to worry about traffic or finding a parking space. It takes 20 minutes to get to my office. Walking up and down the stairs in the subway stations I use makes me healthy.
Jane	I used to take the bus and transfer to the subway, but it took so long that I was tired before I even got to work. So these days I drive to work.
You	
Your Partner	

 **Complete the passage with the following words.**

accelerator	turn signal	windshield wipers	locked
ignition	gas station	brake	parked
steering wheel	ticket	rear-view mirror	checked

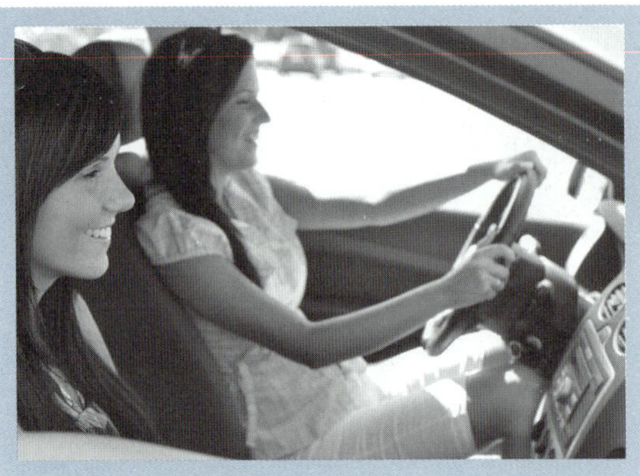

Yuni sat in the driver's seat and her friends sat in the passenger seats. Yuni adjusted her seat and the 1. _______________. She buckled up her seat belt. Yuni put the key into the 2. _______________, turned the key, and started the car.

Yuni started to drive her car. To go faster, Yuni pressed the 3. _______________. As the car sped up, she shifted into a higher gear. To slow down, Yuni let up on the accelerator and shifted into a lower gear. The car slowed down. To stop, Yuni stepped on the 4. _______________. When turning, she put her 5. _______________ on and turned the 6. _______________. When it got dark, she turned on the lights. When it rained, she turned on the 7. _______________.

At intersections, Yuni stopped for red lights. When the lights turned green, she went ahead. Once, she went over the speed limit. A police officer stopped her and gave her a 8. _______________.

Yuni pulled into a 9. _______________ and pulled up to a pump. She told the attendant what kind of gas she wanted and how much. He pumped the gas for her and 10. _______________ the oil. Then she paid him.

At the end of her trip, she 11. _______________ and turned the car off. Yuni and her friends got out of the car and Yuni 12. _______________ it.

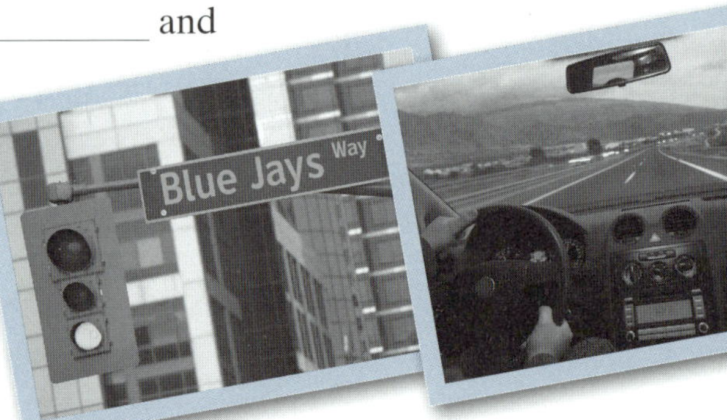

A **Choose the statement which best describes what you see in the picture.** Track 55

(A)   (B)   (C)   (D)

B **Listen to the question and choose the best answer.** Track 56

1. (A)   (B)   (C)
2. (A)   (B)   (C)
3. (A)   (B)   (C)

C **Choose the best answer to each question after listening to the conversation.** Track 57

4. Which statement is true?

   (A) The man wants to get a bus.   (B) The speakers are brother and sister.
   (C) They have not met before.   (D) They are at a subway station.

5. Why is the woman going to Seoul Arts Center?

   (A) To watch a movie   (B) To attend a meeting
   (C) To meet her friends   (D) To go to a concert

Worksheet

Worksheet

Read the clues and write the job using the spaces provided.

1. a person whose job is to keep financial accounts

   ☐ a __ __ __ __ __ __ __ __ __

2. a person who works in business

   ☐ b __ __ __ __ __ __ __ __ __ __ __ __

3. a person who is employed to do office work, such as typing letters, answering phone calls, and arranging meetings

   ☐ s __ __ __ __ __ __ __ __

4. a person who is appointed or elected to a public office, for example working for a local or state government

   ☐ p __ __ __ __ __   s __ __ __ __ __ __

5. a person whose job is to care for people who are ill

   ☐ n __ __ __ __

6. a person who designs buildings

   ☐ a __ __ __ __ __ __ __ __ __

7. a person who plans, designs, and constructs roads, bridges, harbors, and public buildings

   ☐ c __ __ __ __   e __ __ __ __ __ __ __

8. a person whose job involves writing programs for computers

   ☐ c __ __ __ __ __ __ __   p __ __ __ __ __ __ __ __ __

9. a person or business that arranges people's holidays and journeys.

   ☐ t __ __ __ __ __   a __ __ __ __

10. a person who sells things, either in a shop or directly to customers on behalf of a company

   ☐ s __ __ __ __ __ __ __ __ __ __ __

Worksheet

ID # :

NAME :

Put your family photo in the box and describe your family.

ID # :

NAME :

Draw your bedroom or the house which you would like to have and describe it.

04 Worksheet

ID # : ___________________

NAME : ___________________

Write the following numbers in full.

1. 2,500 ___________________

2. 14,320 ___________________

3. 560,000 ___________________

4. 1,200,000 ___________________

5. 32,000,000 ___________________

6. 157,200,000 ___________________

7. 290,009,000 ___________________

8. 4,321,000 ___________________

9. 2,100,000,000 ___________________

10. 110,200,300,400 ___________________

11. 1,000,000,010 ___________________

12. 1,234,567,890 ___________________

13. 5 1/2 ___________________

14. 0.05 ___________________

15. 1.05 ___________________

16. 25 2/5 ___________________

17. 25.50 ___________________

18. 120.99 ___________________

19. 2 1/5 ___________________

20. 5.005 ___________________

ID # : ______________________

NAME : ______________________

Write your daily schedule in brief.

Weekday

Weekend

ID # : ________________________

NAME : ________________________

👉 **Put the photo of a famous entertainer and describe his(her) clothes.**

07 **Worksheet**

ID # : ___________________________

NAME : ___________________________

👉 **Cook your favorite dish this weekend, write a recipe for it and put the photo.**

Ingredients: ___________________________

____

____

____

Method: ___________________________

____

____

____

____

08 Worksheet

ID # : ______________________

NAME : ______________________

☞ **Make an invitation for your birthday party. Give directions to your house.**

How to find my house:

____

____

____

____

____

____

____

____

ID # :

NAME :

Write the terms in English.

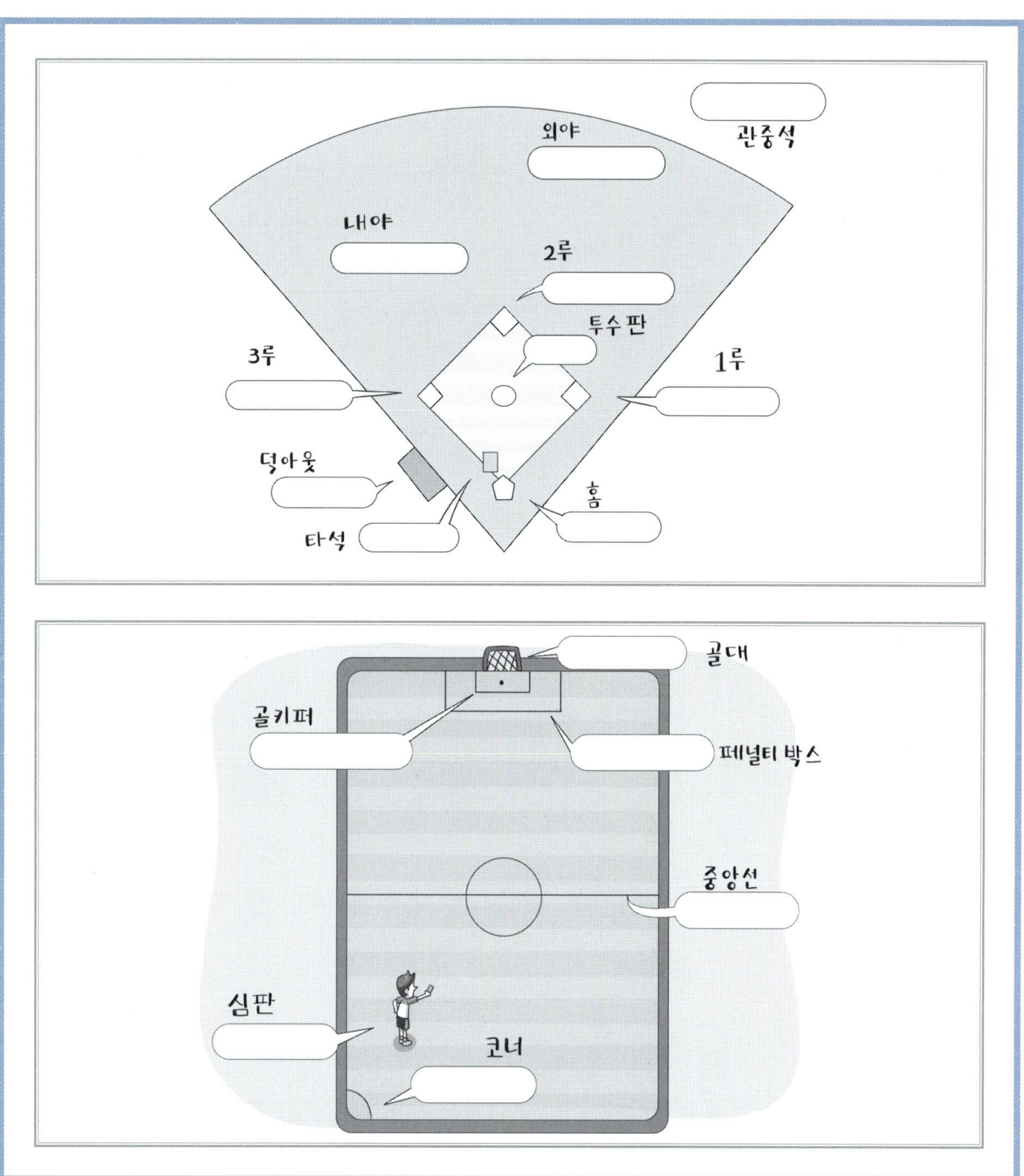

ID # : _______________________

NAME : _______________________

Write the proper words.

Merry Christmas!

ID # :

NAME :

 **Complete the crossword puzzle.**

ACROSS

2. To move an object on screen
4. Pointing device that allows you to tell the computer what to do
5. To remove an item of data from a file or to remove a file from the disk
6. To select an object by pressing the mouse button when the cursor is pointing to the icon

DOWN

1. Electronic junk mail, often an advertisement to many people
3. To press the mouse button twice

Worksheet

ID # : _______________________

NAME : _______________________

👈 Correct the following broken English.

자주 쓰는 한국어	Broken English	Correct Expression
1. 백미러	back mirror	
2. 주유소	oil bank	
3. 와이퍼	wiper	
4. 핸들	handle	
5. 교통위반 딱지	sticker	
6. 레미콘	remicon	
7. 미등	small light	
8. 타이어 펑크	punk tire	
9. 사이드브레이크	side brake	
10. 썬팅	sunting	
11. 오픈카	open car	
12. 카센터	car center	
13. 클락션	klaxon	
14. 휘발유	oil	
15. 휠캡	wheel cap	
16. 본네트	bonnet	

이순향 (Lee, Soonhyang)

중앙대학교 사범대학 영어교육학과 학사
중앙대학교 영어영문학과 석,박사 (음성학 전공)
(현) 부천대학 행정과 부교수

저서: Business Letters

Practical
Campus English
Daily Life

지은이 이순향
펴낸이 정규도
펴낸곳 (주)다락원

초판 1쇄 발행 2010년 2월 25일
초판 3쇄 발행 2017년 2월 21일

책임편집 오수민, 정소연, 김현
디자인 정현석, 함동춘

다락원 경기도 파주시 문발로 211
내용문의 : (02)736-2031 내선 552
구입문의 : (02)736-2031 내선 250~252
Fax (02)732-2037
출판등록 1977년 9월 16일 제 300-1977-23호

값 **10,000**원 (교재 + Audio CD 1개)

ISBN 978-89-277-0005-0 18740

http://www.darakwon.co.kr
다락원 홈페이지를 방문하시면 상세한 출판정보와 함께 동영상강좌,
MP3자료 등 다양한 어학 정보를 얻으실 수 있습니다.